ENDO

Steve Stewart has been doing the Kingdom Discipleship contained in this book longer than most have had any sense of the revelation of it. A seasoned practitioner, Steve sounds a trumpet call to return to the Biblical method of discipleship as demonstrated by the greatest disciple maker of all time, Jesus Christ. As an Apostolic father recognized in more nations than it bears mentioning, Steve's inspired practice-based teaching has equipped saints all over the world to see the kingdom of God advance in unprecedented measure.

The precious gems contained in this book have emerged out of the heart of a fathering elder whose global influence could never be adequately quantified. Why not accept Holy Spirit's invitation to become a disciple maker that influences nations?

Craig Stephens
Territorial Envoy – The Salvation Army, NSW Central Coast
Australia

"Steve Stewart has my ear. "Making disciples" has so often been a banal Evangelical platitude (at least they tried), but Steve's remarkable track record of intentionally and naturally living this message to great effect gives his counsel integrity. In this book, we learn how discipling in community 'works' from someone who's actually and fruitfully practiced Jesus' commission across the globe."

Brad Jersak,
Dean of Ministry Studies, St. Stephen's University
Author of A More Christlike God.

Steve Stewart's newest book is amazing. *The First Church Restored* is very Christ-centered and full of Biblical truth. It is also full of practical instruction and supernatural experience from more than 40 years of ministry experience. Steve will help you both become a disciple and make disciples. If you are hungry for Jesus and you are willing to be a part of what Jesus is doing, this book will help you to move forward in the kingdom. Wherever you find yourself Steve will call you forward.

Adam LiVecchi
Founder of We See Jesus Ministries
Lead Pastor of Rescue Church, Author of Go Preach Heal

What would happen if every time Jesus said to us, "Come and Follow me," — we did? We would turn into Steve Stewart. Steve has spent a lifetime listening to Jesus speak those words "Come follow me," and the following has taken him to the Roma in Bulgaria, the slums of India, and the poor in His own home town. And through it all Steve made a remarkable discovery—There was Jesus already manifesting His kingdom, everywhere Steve put His foot. But this book is far more than that, it is far more than listening to another man's story of following Jesus. It is a practical "how to" by a spiritual father who has been taught by the Lord to see the Kingdom, to live in the Kingdom, and now give all that how to knowledge of the Kingdom away to all those who desire to hear Jesus say "Come and Follow Me."

Murray Dueck
President of Samuel's Mantle Training Society

Steve Stewart is a man after God's own heart. He has written a book that's a must-read for anyone who wants to live the great commission with a great commandment heart.

Leif Hetland
President, Global Mission Awareness, Author of Giant Slayers

I went with Steve Stewart on a "Journey of Compassion" to India where a group of 30 of us ministered and prayed in communities which did not have a church or even electricity. Steve had promised that if I went, I would see people healed as I prayed for them. All 30 in our group experienced the power of God to heal through us when we prayed. That trip to India with Steve changed my life.

Steve tells in his new book, *The First Church Restored*, how his life has been changed by what he has experienced in India. Steve too hungered for more than what was being offered in Western Christianity. Steve met Randeep Mathews and his movement of 800,000 people stretching across northern India. They are living a Christian lifestyle that is MORE and radically different from Western Christianity. Their network of 18,000 house churches is growing rapidly every single day. Steve explains in depth what this MORE is so you and I can embrace it, be stretched by it and experience it.

Answers to your hunger for MORE will be found in these pages. Thank you, Steve.

Dr. Mark Virkler
President – Christian Leadership University and Communion
With God Ministries

I've read a few books that hooked me deep down into my soul—books that transformed me more than just informed me. This is one of those books. This is more of a magnet than just a book. I sensed the draw of the Kingdom of God once again.

Read. Soak. Then give your copy away as soon as possible! I believe the Spirit of God will nudge them as he will you.

Steve Sjogren
Pastor Emeritus, Vineyard Cincinnati
Author, Conspiracy of Kindness
Kindness.com

In *The First Church Restored*, Steve is sharing many powerful insights that are distilled out of over 30 years of ministry. Relational discipleship, where one leads and explains the way to effective ministry rather than merely pointing the way, will prove to be very much more fruitful. In addition, creating ministry opportunities for your disciples is so much more productive than mere instruction. Read this book, put it in practice, and discover for yourself that God can indeed use you as well.

John Arnott
Catch the Fire, Toronto

THE
FIRST CHURCH
Restored

Ancient Truths for
Joyful Discipleship Today

STEVE STEWART

THE FIRST CHURCH RESTORED

Ancient Truths for Joyful Discipleship Today

ESV	English Standard Version
CSB	Christian Standard Bible
TPT	The Passion Translation
NKJV	New King James Version
NCV	New Century Version
CEV	Contemporary English Version
NLT	New Living Translation
MSG	The Message
NRSV	New Revised Standard Version

To contact the author or order copies, visit www.impactnations.org

ISBN: 9781099643613

Library Archives of Canada Cataloguing in Publication available on request

Impact Nations International Ministries, Inc.
PO Box 45596
Rio Rancho, NM 87124

DEDICATION

To Randeep and Anu Mathews:

I dedicate this book to you. What the Lord has done through your lives is truly astounding. Thank you for your great faith in always following Him, wherever He takes you. It is a delight to witness the great joy with which you serve Jesus, a joy that is infectious to all those around you. Thank you for partnering with me and the Impact Nations team to rescue so many lives. Thank you for teaching me that the same joy and abundance that was the everyday life of the first church, is still fully available today. One of the great privileges and joys of my life is to call you my spiritual son and daughter.

TABLE OF CONTENTS

Foreword.. *xi*

Preface...*xv*

1. Recovering The Treasure *1*

2. The Core Agenda *9*

3. What is a Disciple? *29*

4. How Did Jesus Make Disciples? Part One *49*

5. How Did Jesus Make Disciples? Part Two *69*

6. A Turning Point *81*

7. The Early Church: How it all began..............................*91*

8. What Makes a First Church? Part One *111*

9. What Makes a First Church? Part Two..........................*133*

10. Luke 10: The Central Strategy *149*

11. Spiritual Gifts in First Church.................................*167*

12. Hospitality: The Missing Missional Ingredient *181*

13. What to Teach a Disciple *197*

14. It's Time..*215*

Foreword
Steve Sjogren

IT'S SIMPLY PROFOUND

Life is too short to waste time on books that aren't worth reading. My aim is to only read ones that are good enough to re-read. The challenge is that you can't tell in advance if a book really is one of these. *The First Church Restored* is one of those titles.

Steve's message is a tool for God's ongoing realignment to the very core way I see the spread of the gospel of Jesus – that is, to bring a powerful gospel in practical ways. That's pretty much Jesus' entire strategy for bringing his kingdom to planet earth. Through Steve's experience of working with the house church movement overseas, he presents clear and simple ways in which to apply the powerful principles of the early church in today's world.

Something happened to me early in our marriage that stripped the appearance of complication away from any sense of intimidation connected with Jesus' calling.

It was during a strategically important time in our marriage, when several ministry doors were open to us. We saw pros as well as cons in each but there was no clear direction. I was working three jobs to keep body and soul together for our little family. One day, as I was reading a bit of scripture, I saw a ticker tape of sorts go across my mind's eye that said, "Isaiah chapter 61 is for you."

As I read those verses in Isaiah 61 there was a "one-two punch": I was to do the simple, replicable things that Jesus did.

- bringing the good news to the poor
- healing the brokenhearted
- reclaiming liberty to the captives
- to proclaim the year of the Lord's favor
- to comfort those who mourn

As I did those things, His needed power and presence came.

I realized that it was the same calling that Jesus had. My way of walking it out was unique to Janie and me—specifically we planted churches in a variety of places around the world as well as sent out and coached church plants quite different than us.

We've seen time and again that as we do the simple things that Jesus did, His power and presence meet us—the two elements that are necessary for change to happen in any life—whether ours or those we nudge into God's presence by doing the things that Jesus did.

Steve Stewart has been a friend for decades. He and Impact Nations have done the simple yet profound works of Jesus as much as anyone I know around the world. This book presents a gentle but profound message to call you forward as it did to me.

Many years ago, Steve traveled down to spend the weekend with us in Cincinnati Ohio. After a couple of days of practical ministry such as feeding those in need, feeding hungry parking meters, bringing clothes to the projects, there was no getting around it: as we did these and other simple things to serve and bring help, God met us in unmistakable ways. People were healed physically, emotionally, and perhaps even mentally, as we did the little things that Jesus was about and combined them with a yearning to see God's presence and power touch people. As we did that, it was like harvesting low hanging fruit— without a lot of effort required to be fruitful.

As he was leaving, Steve's words to me were, "That's it?" He seemed a little bit disappointed as he boarded the flight home, but as he pondered things on the flight those words echoed back but with a different punctuation, and a powerful clarification. It went from "that's it?" to, "that's it!"

It really is that simple.

Steve Sjogren

Preface

You are holding in your hand a book that traces how Jesus made disciples, how He handed these truths to the apostles and the early church, and how these have been rediscovered in our day. The result is networks of disciple-making house churches that are growing and multiplying faster than at any time in history. *The First Church Restored* is not based on theory; it is not a collection of ideas that *should* work, given just the right conditions. No, this book contains truths which are currently transforming entire regions, and even nations, with the unleashed power of the Gospel of Christ and His Kingdom.

Where the church is exploding around the world, it is *not* because of its mastery of theological principles, or church growth theories. The church is seeing hundreds and even thousands of new disciples every day because it is *living* the way the first century church lived. These churches have uncovered timeless truths that reflect how Jesus lived and how He told us to live. These truths are more than values; they reflect another Kingdom, unlocking its power, its abundance, and its joy. The early church was marked by passionate love for Jesus and for one another. Its corporate life expressed so much vitality, joy and love that daily, people joined this new way of living. And it is the same today. Within the pages of this book you will not only witness what is happening right now, you will see how easy it is to apply these same truths no matter where you are.

As I have ministered in churches and observed church life in over twenty-five nations, I have come to the conclusion that the most effective model for embracing what Jesus taught and lived, is the house church model. However, as I point out in this book, many of the concepts are easily applicable in any small group model.

In a number of ways, the term *house church* is problematic. In the western context, too often house churches are somewhat insular, with the common denominator among the members being their rejection of the traditional church model. Rather than being missional in focus, house churches can become places for wounded believers to come together for support. Beyond this, when house churches gather, they often mirror the Sunday morning meeting. However, *house churches are not a meeting—they are a family*. Families are not defined by a time or place. Wherever they are, or whatever they are doing, a family is always a family.

Preface

Because of common suppositions among western Christians of what a house church is, I have decided to use a different term throughout this book: *First Church*. This reflects the vitality, the fruitfulness, the depth, and the sheer joy of life lived as a Jesus-centered community. What was available to the early church is available to us today.

First Church is not something to think about; it is something to put into practice.

Steve Stewart

1

Recovering The Treasure

"Therefore, every scribe who has been trained
for the kingdom of heaven is like the
master of a household who brings out of his
treasure what is new and what is old."

Matthew 13:52

I simply had to write this book.

Like the man who found the treasure, I have, after a decades-long journey, discovered what Christ promised: abundant life. It is a life shared by those who have also found the treasure. This is a life filled with the joy of experiencing loving community with brothers and sisters, and the profound satisfaction of living with the central purpose of God's Great Story: to reconcile all of creation to Himself.

In 1984 I read *The Early Church* by Gene Edwards. I remember being so bothered by it that at one point I actually threw the book across the room. It challenged so many assumptions about how church was to be done. But after my initial resistance, I was surprised to discover that something else was emerging— hunger. A quiet voice in the back of my mind was starting to get louder: there has got to be more to Christianity than I was experiencing. After the initial blush of joining a thriving charismatic church in the 1970's, slowly yet persistently, a dissatisfaction started to grow. This uneasiness wasn't enough for me to stop going to church on Sunday mornings or be part of a home group, but it was a voice that wouldn't completely go away, no matter how involved in church life I was. There was something missing, but I didn't know what it was.

Shortly after reading the Gene Edwards book, I remember a coffee-room conversation with a few friends at the Christian school where I worked. We talked briefly about our common desire to go deeper in our walk with the Lord and with others. Spontaneously, I invited them to come over that evening to talk some more. When I told my wife they were coming, she asked how many to expect; I told her maybe five or six people. Twenty-five showed up. We talked for hours about what deeper community life could look like. We had no real language to express our longings; ultimately, nothing concrete came from that evening. However, it showed me that I wasn't alone in my desire to see something much deeper in my church experience.

And so, without even being consciously aware that it had begun, I embarked on an expedition that would last, on and off, for more than twenty-five years. I was on a quest to find a kind of church life that reflected the joy and incredible fruitfulness of the first Christians. Many times along the way, I was informed that what the early church lived and experienced was for *then*; after all, we live in a different time and so we have a different wineskin. That always sounded so reasonable—and yet...

My search began in the New Testament scriptures where the Gospels, Acts, and the various letters to the churches of the first century revealed the great joys and challenges of early church life. My love of history led me to study how the church developed from its earliest years, through the middle ages, and through the Reformation and beyond to our day. I studied many church models, especially the various small group strategies and structures that have been written about in so many books and manuals. I observed small groups of various types in Canada, the US, Singapore, and Brazil. They were all interesting and I learned new things wherever I went. But deep down, I knew I still hadn't found what I was looking for (to quote U2).

Then in 2012, while leading a mission team in India, I met a man who introduced me to people who were living a different kind of Christianity than I had ever encountered. It was a model with different strategies, priorities, and values, but much more than these things, what I saw was a new kind of corporate life. I was reminded of the early church father, Tertullian: "Look! How they love one another!" My journey of discovery led me to travel over 2700 kilometers, visiting house churches in rural villages, urban slums, farms and upper-middle class neighborhoods. I remember calling home and telling my wife, "I've found it! At long last I've found it!"

This is a book that seeks to unwrap what I discovered. In the subsequent years, as I continue to engage deeply with the men and women that I met back then, my conviction that there really *is* something more to following Jesus has only increased. I am writing this book largely as a result of my relationship with my spiritual son, Randeep Mathews. Many years ago, He and his wife Anu discovered how to live the rich, shared life of Christ. This discovery has, at this writing, led to over 800,000 people not only coming *to* Christ but learning to live *in* Him. What I have discovered is a movement of people that is networked in over 18,000 house churches stretching across northern India and growing rapidly every single day. It is marked by a deep commitment to the Great Commission (Mt 28:18-20), by remarkable gatherings where every person contributes, by unparalleled evangelistic fruit, and by healthy and growing leadership. But as compelling as all these characteristics are, what has drawn me to these people is witnessing and partaking in a richness of life, a mutual devotion to one another and to Jesus, and an almost unfathomable love that flows back and forth between Jesus and them.

Contained within this model, that I am calling *First Church*, lie principles that unlock the remarkable fruitfulness that the early church discovered. These principles are, therefore, not just for a particular culture. (For example, as I write this, we are watching the Lord move powerfully in Bulgaria among the Roma people, who are embracing the same truths.) This book is for everyone who longs to see new life and fruitfulness flow into their small group and church experience. It is for those who hunger for something deeper, more authentically Biblical, reflecting the life and experience of the early Christians. *The First Church Restored* is for all who have a deep longing to see the men and women in their world meet Jesus and have their lives radically transformed by Him.

A good deal of my time is spent teaching pastors, leaders, and church members in a variety of nations. In the majority of cases, I am talking to men and women who are committed to a more traditional church model. However, over the years it has become clear that many of the principles written about in this book function very well within traditional models. On numerous occasions pastors have reported that after applying many of these principles—even the ones that greatly stretched them out of their comfort zones—their churches flourished.

At the heart of this book are the final instructions of Jesus in both Matthew and Mark, what we call *The Great Commission*. Jesus did not tell us to make house churches nor any particular church model for that matter. He told us go and make *disciples*. I am convinced that the First Church model is the best way to accomplish that goal,

> First Churches live their lives with radical inclusiveness and with a great sense of purpose; they know that Jesus has told them to "go and make disciples".

but it is simply one type of container. If we are to remain faithful to His commands, the "what" of the Gospel is not negotiable; however, the "how" always is. I am personally witnessing the First Church model flourish in much of the developing world. However, I recognize that there are a variety of small group structures and models currently being practiced in the western church. The principles that are illustrated and discussed in this book are readily applicable in all small group models. I know this to be true through my coaching of small group leaders in Canada, the US, and Australia. Whether you are a church planter looking for a new model for our 21st century world, or an established pastor or leader working with small groups within your church, there are proven principles here that can help you on your journey toward making disciples.

Though there is a strong tendency in most of us to cut to the chase, to find out *what* we are supposed to do to make things happen, first the *why* needs to be understood. When we grasp the values and priorities, we have a framework for evaluating, modifying, and applying our strategies and methodologies where the Lord has placed each of us. I am convinced that, no matter where we are, there is a harvest waiting (Jn 4:35). This is because the Creator has "put eternity in the heart of every person" (Eccl 3:11); everyone is made for Jesus and the abundant life of His Kingdom. As His disciples, our heaven-sent assignment is to connect the individuals and families around us to that ultimate reality.

First Churches live with two motivations: nurture and mission. They know that both are needed. God has created us for family, not meetings. First Churches are not defined by a time and place—they are not meetings. Rather, they are living, organic expressions of the body of Christ. First Churches are *people* who, together, are experiencing the joy and fulfillment of being *in Christ*. This is true whether they are in a home, in the park, or sitting in a restaurant. Wherever they are, they are the church. They are people who help one another to truly follow Jesus, to go where He goes and do what He does *every day*. First Churches live their lives with radical inclusiveness and with a great sense of purpose; they know that Jesus has told them to "go and make disciples". These men and women have discovered the "treasure in the field" (Mt 13:44) and their great joy is to share this treasure with everyone.

Jesus repeatedly invited His listeners into an abundant life filled with great joy and fulfillment. This is precisely what I have encountered over the past number of years as I have pursued, witnessed, participated in, and established house churches. For all who have found themselves thinking, "There has to be more", here is some very good news: Yes, there is so much more!

2

The Core Agenda

"Go...and make disciples"

Matthew 28:19

God has created every person on this planet, regardless of ethnicity or religion, with two great needs: security and significance. These are part of our DNA, the Creator's stamp upon our lives. Largely, the 21st century church has done well in meeting the first need. Many churches have a variety of programs to help connect and care for their members: recovery and support classes, men's and women's gatherings, a variety of small groups etc. These are all very good and important; healthy fellowship plays an essential and vital role in our journey with the Lord. As John Wesley once wrote, "There is nothing so *un-Christian* as a solitary Christian." Authentic relationship is not possible without real fellowship. Relationship is the fruit of spending meaningful time together.

However, the other great universal need—significance—has too rarely been emphasized in the western church. This oversight ignores the primal need for our lives to make a difference, to have a purpose outside of, and bigger, than ourselves. I am convinced that this "blind spot" is one of the primary reasons for the numerical and influential decline in the contemporary church. For many believers, good worship and teaching on a Sunday morning is simply not enough. This is reflected in current North American church statistics; 150 churches are closing every week and church attendance is now only 17.7%.[1] I am reminded of what a newcomer to our church once said to me: "After all these years, it is so exciting to find out there is something we can *do* with our Christian faith." Over the past fifteen years, I have watched awakening happen again and again as we have taken men and women out to the front lines of ministry where they can, often for the first time, do the Gospel.

> The Great Commission is not one more thing we should do; rather it is the gateway to discovernig purpose, fruitfulness, and deep joy. If ever there was good news, the Great Commission is it.

In His final words to the disciples in Matthew's account, Jesus addressed this universal human need by aligning us with God's great overarching desire: the reconciliation of all creation (Col 1:20). The Great Commission is not only Jesus' final instruction; it is a declaration of His core agenda for the church.

"All authority in heaven and on earth has been given

[1] https://churchleaders.com/pastors/pastor-articles/139575-7-startling-facts-an-up-close-look-at-church-attendance-in-america.html

to me. Go therefore and make disciples of all nations, baptizing them in the name of the Father and of the Son and of the Holy Spirit, and teaching them to obey everything that I have commanded you. And remember, I am with you always, to the end of the age."

(Mt 28:18-20 CSB)

The Great Commission is not one more thing we should do; rather, it is the gateway to discovering purpose, fruitfulness, and deep *joy*. If ever there was good news, the Great Commission is it. Learning to follow these final words of Jesus has radically transformed my life and the lives of so many around me. Through the Great Commission, I have discovered the treasure in the field—deep relationships in Christ's family with men and women around the world. This is a profound heart-to-heart connectedness that comes from being joined in a common purpose, cosmic and eternal in scope. In His great wisdom, Jesus has given us the destination, and the roadmap to reach it, that gives our lives ultimate meaning. Again, the Great Commission is really, really Good News.

At this point, I encourage you to shift your thinking from house church or some other small group structure. Remember, these are simply vehicles or containers—the "how"—for fulfilling what Jesus has given us to do. In fact, I believe that a more accurate term for house church movement is actually *disciple-making movement*. If we don't understand or remember why we are doing something, it is all too easy to lose sight of the goal. The Great Commission gives us clear instructions and guidelines that keep us steadfastly focused on our assignment

11

from Jesus.

ALL AUTHORITY

The foundation for the commission is that we are operating under the authority of Jesus. His authority is unlike that of any other. It is without limit. It is beyond all time, space and matter. His authority holds all of the universe together. As Paul wrote in his great hymn about Christ,

> [I]n him all things in heaven and on earth were created, things visible and invisible, whether thrones or dominions or rulers or powers—all things have been created through him and for him. He himself is before all things, and in him all things hold together.
>
> (Col 1:16-17 NRSV)

For over three years, the disciples lived their lives with Jesus; progressively, they discovered the vastness of His authority over sickness and infirmity, the powers of darkness, and even the elements. No wonder they said among themselves, "What kind of man is this?" Jesus Christ holds *all* things together. While He was healing the blind and the lame, while He was feeding the 5,000, *at the same time* He was holding the entire cosmos together. We will never fully realize the magnitude of Christ, the second Person of the Triune God.

This is the One who has given us authority to follow in His footsteps, to carry out His purposes on the earth. The Great Commission is not a good idea, plan or strategy. It is His purpose done with His authority. And His authority always comes with favor. As the disciples kept their eyes on Jesus, as they stayed in the center of His assignment, they experienced supernatural blessing. It is this favor beyond the natural realm that lifted them from the obscurity of small villages in occupied Palestine to men who shaped and changed history around the known world. Not their ability; not their personalities—only the authority and favor of God could accomplish this.

I will say it again: God's assignment always comes with divine favor. Following Jesus has connected me with governors, prime ministers, generals, vice presidents, and the man over the five east African nations. Not once have I contacted them. (In most cases, I didn't even know of their existence.) Again, and again, these leaders have contacted me. This has led to thousands of prisoners being released, hundreds of thousands of people being given clean water, being accompanied by the army as we took the Gospel into territory controlled by militant rebels, and all kinds of doors being opened. These are just some examples of the divine favor that comes with the Great Commission. When I am at home in the U.S., I never meet anyone in government or other positions of power. It is because at home, I don't need to. The favor isn't about me; it's about Him. So, when you begin to follow Jesus into this wonderful, joyful and powerful commission, get prepared to see His favor flow to you and through you.

GO

Jesus' commission begins with one emphatic word: "Go". This

simple word presents both a challenge and a paradigm shift for most of us in the church. We have been inculcated with a "come" gospel. For years we have heard, "Come to church. Come to the special meeting. Come to the church concert." Even a cursory reading of the Gospels quickly illustrates that Jesus' message was about *going*. As I have written elsewhere, Jesus lived as the seeking and inviting King. Realistically, very few people will come to church if invited, especially if they have seldom done so in the past. But Jesus told the disciples to go to where the people are. The early church understood this and therefore, lived the gospel out in the marketplace. In the book of Acts, there are 22 miracles recorded; 21 of them happened out in the marketplace. This is clear evidence that the early church understood and were activated by the "Go" of Jesus' final words.

His command to "Go" immediately raises a fundamental question: "Go where?" If you send me on an errand, I can't fulfill that errand until you tell me where to go. This may seem obvious, but it is all too easy to get excited and head out somewhere without Jesus actually directing us. From the beginning, therefore, Jesus' command presses us into learning to listen to His voice. In this way, "Go" is highly relational.

Recently in India, I saw this principle demonstrated perhaps more clearly than I had ever before experienced. Our team of people from around the world was supposed to minister at a colony for beggars. Just as we were about to begin, the heavens opened with torrential rain. In a minute the dirt laneways began to turn into a quagmire; of course, the beggars ran for shelter.

Disappointed, we headed back to our hotel. The rain let up and we decided to go out to a village to prayer walk; but first, our partner Randeep taught about how we can only go *after* we know where to go. While Randeep taught us, his team members gathered to pray and ask Jesus where He was going. At the end of the teaching, they told us that the Lord had given three of them the same place to go. It was a village where none of them had ever been.

Now that we had the name of the village, I assumed that we would go and knock on doors, offering to pray. This was my "do" paradigm. Instead, Randeep had us break into groups of two or three and scatter through the village with two assignments: to bind any spiritual oppression that we sensed, and to ask the Lord to reveal a house of peace—that is, a place that He had prepared beforehand. We went out, praying quietly. Over the next hour, our various teams were invited into nine houses. In each case, the people came out to us, inviting us in for tea and snacks. Everyone reported the incredible hospitality of the people. Most said that they spent much of the time laughing and telling stories together. In the midst of this atmosphere healing, salvation and even deliverance were happening all over the village. Several days later, Randeep's team went back. Healing broke out in house after house. As Randeep told us, "This village will never be the same." This is the fruit of listening.

MAKE DISCIPLES

Jesus told them to *make disciples* as they went. Not converts. Not win souls. Not church members. Disciples. As we will

15

examine in the next chapter, this issue is critical. The church's misunderstanding of this has disempowered the church, resulting in limited or no impact on society. Making disciples is entirely different from having someone put up their hand in a meeting or repeat a prayer, practices that would not have even been comprehended by the early church

Notice to whom Jesus gave the instruction: He gave it to the disciples. They were disciples who were commissioned to make disciples. Logically, therefore, if we are not making disciples, then we are not disciples. Disciples make disciples. I can be a pastor, a home group leader, a teacher of the Scriptures or an elder. Those are all good. But if I am not actually making a disciple, then I am not a disciple. This is a very specific directive, with a very specific goal. I don't make disciples in some general sense (e.g. "I teach people, therefore I am making disciples."); obedience to Jesus' example requires a very specific response.

For this reason, I structure my life to meet with particular individuals on a very regular basis, whereby I can provide specific discipleship. A number of my disciples live overseas, but in our electronic era, that is not too difficult a problem; we meet "face-to-face" on our smart phones, tablets or computers. The Great Commission's directive to make disciples challenges me to always be working with specific people, helping them on their journey as they learn to follow Christ.

In John 12: 26, Jesus said,

"If you want to be my disciple, follow me and you will

go where I am going."(TPT)

Disciples do what Jesus does. They go where He goes—and He is always on the move, going to the lonely, the distressed, the sick and the poor. No wonder it is a "Go" gospel.

We are called to make disciples of Jesus. They are not our church or small group members; they are disciples. We need to think, pray and talk disciples, not members. Disciples change the world. They release the reality of the Kingdom of God. All too often, we think of church members as ours, as those we need to hold onto. Disciples belong to Jesus. We encourage and challenge them, but we don't restrict or control them. Long ago I learned as a pastor that the longer we keep people in the chairs, the harder it is to get them out of the chairs. I also learned to never do ministry by myself; for years I have always taken someone with me to watch, learn and do. This is a vital and practical part of making disciples.

ALL NATIONS

Then Jesus gives a focus for disciple making: *all nations*. This is the great missionary charge of the Gospels. Jesus never doubted that eventually, this would indeed be carried out. That is why He prophesied in Mt. 24:14.

> *"This gospel of the Kingdom will be preached in the whole world as a testimony to all nations, and then the end will come." (NIV)*

As one who leads a mission organization that goes all over the world, I personally understand the international imperative of Jesus' words. But I think there is a more local application. What Jesus actually said was, "make disciples of all *ethnos*". That is, all people groups, all ethnicities. This of course includes nations, and yet goes beyond that. As part of the rapid urbanization of the world's population, most nations have become extremely multi-cultural. Many larger cities have virtually every nation of the world represented within their boundaries; therefore, for most believers, fulfilling this aspect of the Great Commission no longer requires going overseas. Ironically, although they have come from far away, most new immigrants live as isolated from our cultures as before they left their home countries. I was oblivious to their isolation and loneliness until I started to intentionally reach out. Time and again, as we invited people from other nations into our home (some of whom had lived in our country for over ten years), we heard that ours was the first "white" person's home they had ever been in. Inevitably, these new members of our society are eager (but usually shy) to connect, to make friends, to gain a greater understanding of the culture that they now find themselves in. For some of us, going to all nations means getting on an airplane; for others, it means heading across town. But in both cases, disciples "go".

BAPTIZING

"Baptizing them in the name of the Father, the Son and the Holy Spirit." Over the years of teaching pastors and leaders in various countries, I have discovered that this is usually the most contentious portion of Jesus' commission. For most of us in the

evangelical tradition, the model for baptism goes something like this: someone turns to Christ, then they enter a new believer's or baptism class. After several weeks or months, when they have mastered the presented material, they are pronounced ready to be baptized. Sometime following that, they join other candidates as the pastor baptizes each one. Often following the baptism, they are presented with a certificate, commemorating the occasion. The problem is, there is no Biblical evidence for this model. I am not so concerned with whether or not the baptism happens by immersion, or by pouring or sprinkling (as often happened in the eastern early church simply as a by-product of a scarcity of water). The Biblical issues concerning baptism revolve around two questions: When should a person be baptized? Who should do the baptizing?

The book of Acts gives us the clearest picture of how the early church lived, worshiped and ministered. Without exception, when a person came to faith in Christ, they were immediately baptized. From the Ethiopian eunuch who asked Philip, "What would keep me from being baptized?" (Acts 8:36), and Peter with the Roman centurion's entire household, to Lydia and the jailer's household—in every case, when people believed the Gospel, they were immediately baptized. Preparation for baptism through various catechisms only developed at a much later date in church history. I believe that the issue of immediate baptism is critical. Baptism is not merely a ritual; it is a powerful spiritual impartation whereby the Holy Spirit indwells, encourages, teaches and strengthens the new believer. Given this spiritual reality, to delay baptism plays right into our adversary's hand, keeping the new believer from receiving the spiritual impartation that they will so greatly need in the early days of their walk with the Lord. This is borne out by how, almost universally, the enrolment in baptism classes drops as the weeks go by.

According to the Great Commission and the pattern handed down to us by the early church, *who* does the baptizing? Is it the pastor or perhaps a senior elder? No, it is the disciple him or herself who baptizes. Jesus said, "*You* go and make disciples, baptizing them". There is no evidence that the apostles or other leaders did all the baptizing. Just in terms of practicality, when thousands are coming to Christ in a day (Acts 2, 4), it would likely be physically impossible for the twelve leaders of the Jerusalem church to do all the baptizing. A careful reading of First Corinthians reveals that Paul was deliberately downplaying the importance of who did the baptizing; in fact, to avoid any divisions, Paul made a point of baptizing almost no one (1 Cor 1:14,15,17). If Paul is presenting himself as the example, then leaders are clearly not the ones who baptize. So who does? The answer is found in the Great Commission. Those who make a disciple by leading someone to Christ do the baptizing. This was one of the keys to the quick and steady growth of the early church.

Very recently, I had the opportunity to talk to a group of Roma people in Bulgaria about Jesus and His beautiful Gospel. It took place in a small house in a very poor neighbourhood. They received the Good News that Jesus had already accomplished everything for them; now He was inviting them to share His life in and with them. This was received with joy by everyone in the house. That night, I came back with an inflatable pool that I had brought with me from the U.S. There was no running water in the house, and so everyone gathered buckets and large pots and went out into the community, gathering water wherever they could find it. An hour later, in air that was not much above freezing, we baptized the first five people. I baptized the first one, to demonstrate how to do it, then my friends, Steve and Roni, who had already built relationship with the people, baptized the rest. Five days later, in another Roma village, they baptized fifteen more.

For many years Steve and Roni had been members in a traditional evangelical church. During that time, they had seen the pastor occasionally baptize church members, but had never been taught or invited to participate, which of course is the predominant model. Now, they are following the pattern from the early church and the fruit is immediate. Who knows how many Steve and Roni, and those whom they will disciple, will baptize?

TEACHING THEM TO OBEY

"Teaching them to obey everything that I have commanded you."

Up until now, the disciples' job was to watch Jesus, learn from Him, step out and do the ministry themselves. Now it was time for them to go and do it without Him there to supervise. When Jesus sent out the Twelve on their first missionary journey without Him, He said,

"As you go (there's that word again!), *announce this: 'The Kingdom of heaven has come near. Heal the sick, raise the dead, cleanse those with skin diseases, drive out demons."*

(Mt 10:7-8 CSB)

Luke puts it this way:

"He sent them to proclaim the kingdom of God and to heal the sick. So they went out and traveled from village to village, proclaiming the good news and healing everywhere."

(Lu 9:2,6 CSB)

This is the natural progression of discipleship. We can see the disciples' development in ministry, especially through the synoptic Gospels, and then we see the fruit of their learning in Acts. Now, Jesus is declaring the next step of being a disciple: teaching others to do and obey all that they have learned from their time with Him. That is why Acts is largely a record of the disciples testifying and preaching about Jesus—what He did, what He taught and how He died and was resurrected. As Paul said, "I purposed to know nothing among you except Christ" (1 Cor 2:2). This is why it is so important to study and teach others from the record of the four Gospels. If we are going to follow Jesus, we must learn all that we can from Him.

In his final letter, Paul wrote with great urgency to his spiritual son, Timothy:

You have often heard me teach. Now I want you to tell these same things to followers who can be trusted to tell others.

(2 Ti 2:2 CEV)

The disciples stayed true to Jesus' final words to them; year after year, person by person, they faithfully taught others all that they had learned from Him, by both word and demonstration. And always, the directive remained the same: "What I have taught you, in turn, you teach others." Remember, disciples make disciples.

I AM WITH YOU ALWAYS

Jesus last words to His disciples and friends are filled with comfort and encouragement. In John's Gospel, Jesus promises to send them the Holy Spirit as the comforter and teacher. Through the presence of the Holy Spirit, Jesus will never leave them. This promise of His Presence is the final, and perhaps greatest, key of all. For as the disciples stepped out, in spite of any feelings of inadequacy or insecurity, it is in their *going* that He promises to be most closely with them. In Ezekiel's vision of the river flowing from the Temple (Ezek 47), the further away that the river flows, the greater its depth. In following Jesus into His rescuing, reconciling and restoring ministry, it is "out there" where we really need the Holy Spirit's power and presence to be manifested. Remember, with His presence comes His supernatural favor. Making disciples is really a partnership with Jesus. We go, make and baptize disciples, and teach them what it means to follow Him; and He empowers and anoints our actions. In John's Gospel, Jesus calls this fruitfulness. He tells the disciples to bear fruit, because by doing this,

"When you produce much fruit, you are my true disciples. This brings great glory to my Father."

(Jn 15:8 NLT)

Obedience to Jesus' great purpose attracts His presence, anointing, and power. In the early church, everyone could see that "great grace was upon them all" (Acts 4:33). It has always been His presence and purpose that has attracted newcomers. Like the first disciples, as we wholeheartedly embrace the Great Commission, this Magna Carta from our Lord, we enter into His supernatural rhythm where we discover that He does more and does it faster than we ever imagined.

PUTTING IT INTO PRACTICE

Further into this book we will be delving more deeply into the issues raised by Jesus' core agenda; however, the Great Commission provides an excellent framework for beginning to activate some principles. At the end of each chapter you will find some of these principles, and some leading questions to help point the way.

"GO"

1. Contrary to what most of us have experienced, this is a *go* Gospel, not a *come* Gospel. It presents us with both an invitation and a challenge.

2. Before you can go, you have to know where Jesus is sending you. How can you incorporate listening praying into what your group does together? Remember the promise of Jn 10:27: "My sheep hear My voice."

3. What would your First Church or small group need to change in order to implement *going*? Where can you *go* as a group to demonstrate the love of Jesus and the power of His Gospel?

4. How can you make *going* a part of your regular practice?

MAKE DISCIPLES

1. According to Mt 28, disciples make disciples. If you want to be a disciple, then you must be making a disciple.

2. The best way to make a disciple is to find someone who doesn't yet know Jesus and befriend him or her. (We will talk about the power of the "person of peace" later in the book.)

3. The next best way is to find a believer who is younger in the faith. Ask the Holy Spirit who you are to give yourself to. Once you know, ask the Lord to speak to that person. Make yourself available and see what happens. If it is the person the Lord is sending you, he will respond to you; do not pursue him. This needs to be led by the Holy Spirit.

4. Whenever you go out to do ministry, always take a

disciple with you.

5. As a small group or First Church, be encouraging one another to be making disciples.

OF ALL NATIONS

1. As already stated, we live in a time when we can go to the nations right in our own cities. But the Great Commission also calls us to go to the nations.

2. As a First Church, support one or two members to go on a short term mission trip. Not only is the cost shared, the entire group is emotionally and spiritually invested in the Kingdom advancement that takes place.

3. John's third letter presents us with clear instructions about this:

   "You will do well to send them on in a manner worthy of God; for they began their journey for the sake of Christ, accepting no support from non-believers. Therefore, we ought to support such people, so that we may become co-workers with the truth."

   (3 Jn 6-8 CSB)

BAPTISM

1. Instead of a leader or pastor doing the baptizing when a group member leads someone to Christ, have him or her do it. Remember, this was the practice of the early church. If at all possible, have the First Church

participate. Families celebrate together, and a First Church is a family. This can be done in most homes, either in a backyard pool, a bathtub, or even a children's blow-up pool.

2. Most importantly do not have a long delay from the time of turning to Christ to the time of baptizing.

3

What is a Disciple?

"His disciples followed Him."

Matthew 8:23

The final directive of Jesus was to go and make disciples. In the coming chapters we will look at how Jesus specifically modeled this, and then at how we, in community, can go about making disciples as He did. It is important to first look honestly at the results of how we are currently making disciples. After all, Jesus often challenged His listeners to examine the fruit. The first step toward transformation is to recognize the need for change, even when our observations are painful. The point is not to be critical of what the church is doing wrong; rather, it is to help us see that Jesus and the early church lead us in a new and vibrant direction.

Multiple studies have demonstrated that the contemporary church in the West has failed to be a change-agent in our society; in fact, in all too many ways, society has changed the church. The apostolic writers understood the danger:

"Do not love this world nor the things it offers you, for when you love the world, you do not have the love of the Father in you."

(1 Jn 2:15 NLT)

"Dear friends, I warn you as 'temporary residents and foreigners' to keep away from worldly desires that wage war against your very souls."

(1 Pe 2:11 NLT)

One of the foundational qualities of being a disciple of Jesus is living according to His example and standard. Multiple studies conducted in North America that compare the lifestyles of Christians and non-Christians are not encouraging.

The findings in numerous national polls conducted by highly respected pollsters like The Gallup Organization and The Barna Group are simply shocking. "Gallup and Barna," laments evangelical theologian Michael Horton, "hand us survey after survey demonstrating that evangelical Christians are as likely to embrace lifestyles every bit as hedonistic, materialistic, self-centered, and sexually immoral as the world in general." Divorce is more common among "born-again" Christians than in the general American population.[1]

---

1 Ron Sider: The Scandal of the Evengelical Conscience, ChristianityToday, January/February 2005 http://www.christianitytoday.com/bc/2005/001/3.8.html

In Barna's *Second Coming of the Church*, he details some of the statistics that led to his conclusions. Christians are less likely to give to a homeless person or to donate to a non-profit organization than non-Christians. Christians are much more likely to view refugees and immigrants in a negative light, even though the Bible repeatedly directs us to love and care for the alien and the stranger. Rates of employee theft, violence in the home, and divorce all point to one conclusion: many North American Christians do not live as salt and light, or as a city on a hill; in short, not as disciples of Jesus Christ. I believe that this is the result of accepting the Christian faith, but without being intentionally discipled in that faith. It is time to face head-on the results of what we have been doing in the western church. Then, we must make whatever changes are necessary, no matter how uncomfortable, in order to more faithfully follow the way of Jesus. The church of the first three centuries offers us a pattern and standard that greatly illuminate the journey of how Jesus made disciples.

THE STANDARD OF THE EARLY CHURCH

The early church did not merely engage in making disciples; it was *built* upon discipleship as it faithfully sought, year after year, to obey Jesus' Great Commission. The result was a dynamic, resilient, and growing church. In the face of sometimes deadly persecution, ridicule and campaigns of misinformation, the early church flourished. It went from tiny pockets of believers meeting in homes, to the most powerful change agent in history, transforming much of the known world. As Paul said to the Roman church, "The Gospel is the power of God unto salvation" (Ro 1:16).

During the first several centuries of the church, much emphasis was given to learning to live by a particular, countercultural standard, one that was immediately recognized as a radical departure from social norms. As David Bentley Hart has written,

> "When one truly ventures into the world of the first Christians, one enters a company of "radicals" (for want of a better word), an association of men and women guided by faith in a world-altering revelation, and hence in values almost absolutely inverse to the recognized social, political, economic, and religious truths not only of their age, but almost every age of human culture."[2]

The early church embraced the New Testament call to live as strangers and sojourners in this world. There is no way around this: they were committed to a lifestyle that stood out in their own day as deeply countercultural. Yet paradoxically, although disciples lived distinctly, they did not live in isolation. Jesus instructed all who would follow Him to live as penetrating agents in society. Like salt, light and leaven, disciples slowly and patiently, but resolutely, change the atmosphere all around them. Like Jesus, disciples live inclusively, always inviting and caring for the world around them. They are the light that changes the darkness; knowing this, the early church was quietly but steadfastly missional.

---

2   David Bentley Hart, The New Testament (New Haven: Yale University Press, 2017), xxiv

While our post-modern Western worldview leads us to think of discipleship as something for the individual, in the early church discipleship happened primarily in a corporate context. The lives of the believers were centered around their common life as the body of Christ. This corporate faith was each disciple's encouragement and example for living; they intentionally lived by a higher standard. This often put them at odds with the culture around them. Their common life provided the encouragement and support necessary to persevere. In their corporate gatherings (usually in a home), the new believers were discipled; here they learned scripture, how to pray and worship, and how to recognize, receive, and walk in Christ's presence.[3]

The early church's worship services involved more time and focus on prayer and public reading of the scriptures than most of us experience today. In these gatherings, the people were very intentionally being taught how to pray by example, with a lot of responsive prayers. And since individuals did not have Bibles, and the vast majority of people were illiterate, the only way to learn the scriptures was at the worship service. Therefore, much time was given to public reading. The corporate focus on discipleship reminded everyone that each of them are a part of Christ's body. The Eucharist, or Lord's Supper, was the climax of every worship service. Their shared understanding of the service was that through prayer, singing and scripture, the assembled church was progressively ascending toward the Triune God. A central theme of the New Testament writers was reminding the church that they are a whole new creation,

3   https://fmcusa.org/lightandlifemag/how-the-early-church-made-disciples/

a people of the Spirit. One of the clearest examples of how the church understood its ascent through the worship service is found in Hebrews:

> *"You have come to Mount Zion, to the city of the living God, the heavenly Jerusalem, and to countless thousands of angels in a joyful gathering. You have come to the assembly of God's firstborn children, whose names are written in heaven. You have come to God himself, who is the judge over all things. You have come to the spirits of the righteous ones in heaven who have now been made perfect. You have come to Jesus, the one who mediates the new covenant between God and people"*
>
> *(Heb 12:22-24 NLT)*

In the Eucharist, heaven comes down. The believers understood that they were actually receiving the life of Christ afresh each week. In the bread and the wine, they knew that Christ was present in their midst; by taking these elements, they were receiving more of Christ *in* them, and by this, they were being transformed and empowered by His Spirit. This is why the worship service was central to discipleship.

Our contemporary discipleship methodology has largely revolved around teaching a body of information with the understanding that, when mastered, it will lead to transformation. This information is disseminated through books, pulpit teaching, small group material, new believers' classes, and one-on-one meetings. No matter the format, the goal is mastery of a body of information. It is interesting that early church writings reveal that this pull toward teaching as the primary means of discipleship started to develop after just 200 years.

By almost exclusively focusing on discipleship as primarily presenting information, we have formed disciples who have various levels of theoretical knowledge, but very little practical experience of what it means to do what Jesus did. Recently, while spending a few days teaching pastors in Kenya, I told them the following story:

> I led a team to a number of villages in Samar, Philippines, where among other things, we conducted outdoor meetings. During one of these meetings I prayed for a teenager for healing. After being healed, I told her that Jesus had another gift for her—to live inside her forever. She gladly received His gift of new life. Then I asked her to come with me as we walked among the crowd who had come forward. This young lady watched as I followed the same pattern that she had experienced. Again, the person was healed, then invited to embrace the gift of Jesus, which she did. Then we went to someone else and I said to the young lady, "Now you have seen what Jesus does. You pray for healing, then invite them to receive Christ."

At this point, the Bishop of these pastors exclaimed, "That girl learned more that day than I have in 27 years!" I was struck by his honesty and transparency in the midst of his subordinates and peers. If we continue to build our discipleship models primarily upon mastering information, we risk creating theoretical

Christians, not disciples. In contrast, the early church was discipling men and women according to the standard taught to them by the first apostles, who had learned directly from Jesus. This is what Paul meant when he wrote that the church is:

"Built on the foundation of the apostles and prophets with Christ Jesus Himself as the cornerstone."

(Eph 2:20 CSB)

WHAT DID JESUS MEAN BY "DISCIPLE"?

Obviously, in order to understand Jesus' approach to making disciples, we first need to examine what Jesus meant by the term. Disciple (Gr: *mathetes*) literally means a learner and generally refers to a student, apprentice or adherent. Disciple was a common term in the Greek world, and later in both Roman and Jewish society. As Greg Herrick explains,

> [T]here are examples of discipleship referring to people committed to following a great leader, emulating his life and passing on his teachings. In these cases, discipleship meant much more than just the transfer of information. Again, it referred to imitating the teacher's life, inculcating his values, and reproducing his teachings.[4]

The word, "disciple" occurs 232 times in the Gospels and Acts. It is largely used to designate those who followed Jesus; secondly, it is used by Jesus Himself, usually to indicate the

---

4 https://bible.org/seriespage/2-understanding-meaning-term-disciple

qualifications and conditions of being His disciple. If we look at His words honestly, without cushioning them to fit our modern sensibilities, we are faced with how shockingly radical they really were (and still are).

"Then He said to them all, "If anyone wants to follow after Me, let him deny himself utterly, take up his cross daily, and follow Me. For whoever wants to save his life will lose it, but whoever loses his life because of me will save it."

(Lu 9:23-24 ESV)

"If anyone comes to me and does not hate his own father and mother and wife and children and brothers and sisters, yes, and even his own life, he cannot be my disciple.

(Lu 14:26 ESV)

"So therefore, any one of you who does not renounce all that he has cannot be my disciple."

(Lu 14:33 ESV)

The most repeated saying of Jesus in the Gospels is: *"If anyone seeks to save his life, he will lose it. If anyone loses his life for My sake (or the sake of the Gospel), he will find it."* Jesus preached a clear, unyielding message, inviting His listeners into a radical, uncompromising commitment to a whole new way of life that was built upon new beliefs, values and practices. The invitation to follow Jesus, was a call to imitate Him, and in doing so, to make other disciples.

Jesus gave us some clear attributes that mark a disciple as belonging to Him.

1. A disciple loves. *"By this all will know that you are My disciples, if you have love for one another." (Jn 13:35 NKJV)*

2. A disciple is steadfast. *"You are truly my disciples if you remain faithful to my teachings. (Jn 8:31 NLT)*

3. A disciple is fruitful. *"My Father is glorified by this: that you produce much fruit and prove to be my disciples." (Jn 15:8 CSB)*

In Mark's Gospel, Jesus goes up on a mountain to pray regarding who He should appoint to be in His inner circle of disciples. Jesus appointed the disciples for three things: to be with Him, to send them out to preach, and to have authority to drive out demons. It seems that Mark's order here is significant. First and foremost, at the heart of discipleship is deep and authentic relationship with Jesus. Before there is *going*, there must be *being*. Time spent with Jesus is the core of everything for a true disciple; it is this that re-shapes us. It is significant that the Jewish leaders who were accusing Peter and John "recognized that they had been with Jesus" (Acts 4:13). Secondly, Jesus would commission the disciples to *go* with authority to perform signs and wonders, but only after they built a history of *being* with Him. Throughout their years with Jesus, they lived a continual rhythm of being and going.

Even the four Gospels themselves present this balance. Matthew and Mark, the earliest Gospels, culminate in Jesus' final sending, the Great Commission. There is an urgency that cannot be missed. In John's Gospel, written a generation later, there is an emphasis on the necessity to abide, to rest and stay—all captured in the Greek word *meno*, which John uses 63 times in his account. Repeatedly, Jesus calls the disciples to stay close to Him, to draw life from Him. Certainly, Jesus points the disciples to look outward ("lift up your eyes and see, the fields are white unto harvest"), but almost all activity is balanced by abiding in Him.

> *"I am the vine; you are the branches. The one who remains in Me and I in him produces much fruit, because you can do nothing without Me.*
>
> *(Jn 15:5 CSB)*

Look at a grapevine. The branches are so intertwined as to be almost indistinguishable from one another. The early disciples understood abiding in Christ largely in the context of being together with His people. Although in our highly individualized world we often miss this, most of the time in the New Testament, "you" is actually plural. The writers assumed they were primarily addressing the corporate life of disciples.

The new community that formed around Jesus and His message declared through their corporate life that they lived, not just by a different standard, but by a completely new, unheard of orientation. They were focused not on this life, but on the fully realized Kingdom of God which awaited all who would faithfully follow Him. Jesus lifted the vision of many who heard Him, opening up to them a new, eternal perspective. These are the words we love to hear today. But equally, His words tore away many of the moorings on which the early disciples had built their lives.

In the early church, following Jesus was not just a spiritual decision; it radically touched every part of life. At various times during the first 300 years of the church, following Jesus was literally a life-threatening choice. (It is still the same today for many in Asia and the Middle East. I work with partners who have been shot at, stabbed, and left to die; others have had family members martyred, churches bombed, and members killed. Frankly, these realities have affected my response to believers talking and writing about the "persecution" that we face in the West.) Being a disciple meant financial hardship, loss of advancement or employment, loss of social standing, friends and even family. In order to survive, it often meant sharing everything: housing, food, possessions, and money.

And yet...

In spite of these immense difficulties—or perhaps because of them—the church grew rapidly. There was a great attractiveness that drew people into this whole new way to live. In his excellent study of the early church, Alan Kreider writes:

> "[The church] proliferated because the faith that these fishers and hunters embodied was attractive to people who were dissatisfied with their old cultural and religious

habits, who felt pushed to explore new possibilities, and who then encountered Christians who embodied a new manner of life that pulled them toward what the Christians called "rebirth" into a new life."[5]

IT BEGINS WITH FOLLOWING JESUS

It seems obvious that Jesus' first requirement to all those who wanted to be His disciples, was to simply follow Him. Without following Jesus, any concept of discipleship is at best theoretical; I would say that it is, in fact, nonsensical. Jesus said in John 12:26 that if anyone is going to be his servant (disciple) then he must follow Him, and therefore he will be wherever Jesus is. That seems straightforward, so let us examine His first invitation to follow.

One day as Jesus was walking along the shore of the Sea of Galilee, he saw two brothers—Simon, also called Peter, and Andrew—throwing a net into the water, for they fished for a living. Jesus called out to them, "Come, follow me, and I will show you how to fish for people!" And they left their nets at once and followed him.
(Mt 4:18-20 NLT)

Jesus encounters and calls these brothers in the midst of their daily work. Matthew records Jesus doing the same thing with two other fishermen and a tax gatherer. The encounter did not

---

5 Alan Kreider, The Patient Ferment of the Early Church (Grand Rapids MI: Baker Academic, 2016), 12.

happen in the synagogue. Jesus went to them; He didn't wait for them to come to a meeting. He took the initiative. Jesus *called* them, knowing that what will make these men disciples is the power of that call. It is as though their true potential is announced in Jesus' words, but the potential is only unlocked through their immediate response. Their relationship with Jesus began with obedience.

And what did Jesus invite them into? He did *not* say, "If you follow Me, I will lead you to the Father. I will heal your heart of all its pain. If you follow Me, you will go to heaven." No, He said, "Come follow Me, there's a job to do and I am going to teach you how to do it—to fish for people." This was an invitation to effectiveness by Jesus' standard. There is a profoundly countercultural truth in this invitation: Jesus calls disciples to a *useful* life, not a *successful* one. The pursuit of success is the enemy of the Gospel because it changes the basis and reason by which we decide whether or not we will follow Him.

This is critical because it gets to the heart of the invitation of God, what we call evangelism. From the beginning, the disciples understood that the invitation was about mission and a purpose bigger than themselves. It was about losing themselves for the sake of people and God's greater story. And along the way, Jesus led them to the Father, brought deep healing into their lives, and told them that there would come a day when they would be with Him forever. All those things were true, but they were not at the heart of His invitation to follow Him.

What is God's great cosmic purpose? To reconcile all things to Himself (Col 1:20). *This* is what has the power to cause people to drop everything and follow Jesus wherever He went. This cosmic purpose rescues and restores lives. When the disciples saw it, immediately they dropped everything. For us in the West, where we have carefully planned our lives and constructed our safety nets, such a response seems almost mythical. Years of familiarity with these passages has dulled their impact. However, Jesus' words, "Follow Me" have the power to tear men and women away from what had been most precious to them. The power of His words is just as real today.

Luke's version of Jesus' invitation to follow Him reveals another critically important aspect of this call. After preaching to the crowd, Jesus told Peter to go back out fishing; Peter obeyed and a huge, supernatural number of fish were caught.

> *When Simon Peter realized what had happened, he fell to his knees before Jesus and said, "Oh, Lord, please leave me—I'm too much of a sinner to be around you."*
>
> *(Lu 5:8 NLT)*

Jesus response is instructive: He ignored Peter's confession of sin and commissioned him as a disciple.

> *"'Don't be afraid', Jesus told Simon. 'From now on you will be catching people!'"*
>
> *(Lu 5:10 CSB)*

Jesus did not tell Peter to wait until he had dealt with his sin before he could follow. This was true for everyone that Jesus called. Here is the key: there was *no* preparation to becoming a disciple. Character formation, maturity and gifting all took place *in the process* of being a disciple. Far too often, we turn disciples into domesticated church members by making them sit still and learn before they can actually do the works of a disciple. Being a disciple is not about preparation, but *willingness*.

Sometime later, Jesus told the disciples to "pray to the Lord of the harvest to send out workers into His harvest" (Mt 9:37). Whereas others just saw sinners, corrupt officials (including tax gatherers), militant revolutionaries (such as zealots), and illiterate men and women, Jesus saw harvest workers—not potential or future harvest workers. Disciples make disciples, and this begins with seeing everyone as a potential harvest worker.

Following Jesus is the watershed issue of authentic discipleship. As long as we stay where we are, we seek to be disciples on our terms, focusing only on the issues that we want to see changed. Following Him is everything. Jesus never told them to pray or sing songs about following Him, or to consider it for a while. He just said, "follow Me". It was by immediately following Him that their lives were changed. This is so critical. It is only by following Him that we move from theory and comfort into the adventure (and discomfort) of real discipleship.

By and large in our 21st century western Christian culture, we are enamored with the idea of following Jesus, but to *actually* follow is costly. We too often settle for an imitation. We pray about following Him; we sing songs about following Him; we tell ourselves that soon we'll be in a more prepared place to follow Him. But we stay where we are. Here is reality: You can't *go* somewhere until you *leave* somewhere. As Bonhoeffer wrote,

> The call to follow at once produces a new situation. To stay in the old situation makes discipleship impossible. Levi must leave the receipt of custom and Peter his nets in order to follow Jesus...The only right and proper way is quite literally to go with Jesus. The call to follow implies that there is only one way of believing on Jesus Christ, and that is by leaving all and going with the incarnate Son of God.[6]

Furthermore, we are formed through our leaving/following. Jesus continuously moved about Judea and Galilee, always taking His disciples with Him. In new and uncertain places and situations, we are less able to rely on our own strengths and resources. This is one practical way that we experience what John the Baptist declared: "He must increase, and I must decrease."

Following Jesus isn't an attitude, it is a *life* that forms us. It is no different for us than for His first disciples; the essence of following is movement. This movement may be literally relocating to another city or nation (I think He calls us to this

6   Dietrich Bonhoeffer, The Cost of Discipleship, (New York: Touchstone, 1959), 62

more than we like to admit), or it may be a movement to new ministry or outreach. Whatever it is, following Him means movement. And why is this so hard for us? Because we have an enemy, the accuser (Rev 12:9). His strategy is usually quite straightforward. When Jesus says, "Come follow Me", our enemy says, "You're not quite ready yet. Soon." We always get to choose, and no one is forcing our choices. We can keep safe, stay with the familiar and limit our risks, or we can choose to actively trust Jesus when He calls. We can choose mental assent or active obedience.

The factor that tips the scales of our decision is Jesus' great promise: to choose to give up life on our own terms and to follow Him according to His terms, means that we will find the true and abundant life that has always been waiting for us. It is a narrow way, but it is where we find "the treasure hidden in a field" (Mt 13:44).

PUTTING IT INTO PRACTICE

BEING SALT AND LIGHT

1. For disciples in the early church, following Jesus radically touched every part of life. Both as a group and as a focus point for individual contemplation, consider honestly what aspects of your life have been impacted by your decision to follow Jesus. What parts have not?

2. The early church lived distinctly, but not in isolation. This distinctiveness is what made them "a city set on a hill". Jesus used various metaphors to describe how

disciples are to be change agents: salt, light, and leaven. Each of these must be in contact with their surroundings in order to bring about change. Identify the specific contact points that the group has and those of individual members. How can these increase? How can we make the most of these contacts?

3. Consider your small group or First Church as a lighthouse in the neighborhood. Discuss:

- Do we truly stand out as a lighthouse and a safe place in this neighborhood? If this small group closed down, would the neighborhood notice?

- How can we increase our presence in this neighborhood?

LEARNING TO ABIDE

1. "First and foremost, at the heart of discipleship is deep and authentic relationship with Jesus. Before there is *going*, there must be *being*. Time spent with Jesus is the core of everything for a true disciple; it is this that re-shapes us." Intimacy with the Triune God is both the center and the foundation of a disciple's life.

- Intimacy and communication go hand in hand. How can this First Church or small group learn to hear the voice of Jesus when we meet together? (Jn 10:27)

- Discuss both the blessings and challenges that each

one encounters in their time of waiting on the Lord.

FOLLOWING JESUS

1. To be a disciple of Jesus means to *follow* Him; and if we are going to follow Him, we must *be where He is* (Jn 12:26). Being a disciple—following Jesus—means *movement*. It may be physically moving somewhere, or it may be moving from long-held preferences and patterns. In either case, we can't *go* somewhere until we *leave* somewhere.

   • What or where is Jesus calling you to leave? Where is there movement in your life?

   • Is there something that Jesus is calling this group to leave? A familiar way of doing things? A comfortable pattern? Something else?

2. How is our adversary using his strategy of saying, "Soon" in our lives? How can we help one another to follow Jesus' invitation with faith and obedience?

4

How Did Jesus Make Disciples?
Part One

*"He sent them to preach the kingdom of God
and to heal the sick."*

Luke 9:2

Jesus was more effective at making disciples than anyone in history; what He imparted to the men and women who followed Him ultimately changed the world. A careful consideration of Jesus' methods will reveal what we can learn from Him as we seek to effectively make disciples in the 21st century.

At the heart of Jesus' discipleship methodology was formation. Most of our contemporary modes have placed great emphasis upon transferring a body of information from teacher to students, with the hope that this would somehow form disciples. However, by itself, information can be learned and then forgotten without resulting in any significant change. But formation is about deep change: in the way we think and act, what we believe and most value, and how we order our lives. It is about re-forming our core identity—both individually and in a new kind of community.

Jesus formed disciples primarily in three ways: He instructed, He welcomed people to watch Him and imitate what they saw, and He included a group of people to share life with Him. There is much we can learn from each of these three methods.

TEACHING

During his earthly ministry, Jesus was often referred to as "Teacher" or "Rabbi." This was because He was always very public in his teaching and this was most people's initial point of contact. Jesus taught in a variety of settings: with his disciples, often while walking or travelling by boat; in front of large crowds; at the Temple in Jerusalem; even with the various Jewish religious sects.

There are numerous examples in the Gospels of Jesus directly teaching the people. The Sermon on the Mount, the five discourses in Matthew, the Sermon on the Plain (Lu 6) and the Farewell Discourse (Jn 14-16) are perhaps the best examples of Jesus verbally instructing His listeners. It is important to note that when teaching, He always looked beneath surface actions to the motivations of the heart. Jesus knew that real change— formation—came from the inside-out and not the other way around. Religious teaching so often focuses on actions and outcomes, leading to a Gospel that stresses *doing* more than *being*. And, as we saw in the last chapter, the fruit of this kind of instruction has not been good. Much of Jesus' instruction was narrative. He often told parables, stories that used allegory and metaphor to penetrate past rational defenses in order to confront the heart and *prompt a change* in His listeners. This change of heart and mind is called *metanoia*, which most of our Bibles translate as repentance. In contrast, we have largely relied on teaching principles as truth to be understood and considered, believing that this would bring about the desired change in our listeners.

I came to Christ as a young married man. In His wonderful mercy, I encountered Jesus alone in my bedroom. I had no Christian friends and almost no real church experience. Three months after encountering Jesus, I remember finding the courage to walk into a church. I had no frame of reference for what was going on, but in the midst of my confusion and, frankly, discomfort with what I was witnessing, I remember a deep and quiet sense that I was finally home.

For the first couple of years, I was like a sponge. I went to every meeting so I could learn more. I read the Bible and Christian books voraciously. But gradually, I began to feel a sense of uneasiness. Deep down, I was asking myself, is this all there is? Do we just keep doing this until we go to heaven? I think one of the problems was that what we were being taught so rarely connected with my life outside the church. One day, in a moment of great honesty, a friend from church said that he felt as though there was a "teaching pile" that got bigger every week but was never used.

Later, when I had planted my first church, each week as I began each week to work on my sermon outline, the first thing I did was to write a question in block letters at the top of the page: "WHAT DIFFERENCE DOES THIS MAKE?". No matter how interesting a particular point or section of the sermon seemed to me, if it couldn't answer that question, I scratched it out. Jesus' teaching always had direct and obvious application. His stories came from real life. I have always been determined to try and follow His example. That is one reason why, during my many years of planting and pastoring churches, I would go out into the community each week to find opportunities to meet, serve and pray for people. As a result, when I preached each Sunday, I could tell stories from that week in our own city.

> The longer you keep the people in the chairs, the harder it is to get the people out of them.

Sometimes, I would make my teaching practical in ways that would surprise the congregation. On many occasions over the years, before starting to preach, I would tell them that there were 25 food hampers waiting in the foyer. They were going to be taken to a poor neighborhood and given to families. They didn't know we were coming, and we didn't know which doors we would go to—we would have to ask the Holy Spirit. Then I would tell the congregation that, when I counted to three, the first 25 people who came to the front got to *do* the Gospel instead of staying behind and listening to me talk for forty minutes. And the people would actually run to the front. Maybe that was more a comment on my preaching than their desire to minister to people!

At this stage in my life, I often find myself invited to speak at conferences and seminars in various countries. Before agreeing, I always tell the organizers that I would be pleased to speak on one condition: as part of the event, I will take the participants out into the community to put what I have been teaching into practice. Inevitably, the people go out feeling both nervous and skeptical that anything good will happen. Just as inevitably, they return to the conference two hours later filled with excitement as they share with each other their stories of Jesus moving in healing and salvation.

Jesus taught His disciples in a variety of settings: besides speaking to large crowds, much of His teaching was while they were walking, sharing a meal, or traveling by boat. As a result, much of Jesus' teaching arose from the moment to moment situations in which they found themselves. Their shared life provided the opportunity and the canvas for Jesus to present instruction that was immediately relevant and applicable. This fact alone should challenge the limitations of our modern teaching methods which are largely chained to the restrictions of the classroom setting. One of the drawbacks of the traditional teaching model is that it has no real end point. As a result, it tends to lead to a process that implies the disciple isn't quite ready yet. I think that delay is one of our enemy's prime strategies against the church. As I often say to pastors during training events: "The longer you keep the people in the chairs, the harder it is to get the people out of them." Teaching is undoubtedly of great importance, as the New Testament often points out. However, we can follow Jesus' example into much richer, relevant and formative ways to instruct. We need to re-capture the power of teaching as we "walk by the way" (Dt 11:19), rather than always in the more predictable (and safer) setting of the classroom. In contrast, effective, formative disciple-making often happens in the movement of life. Learning to recognize the "teachable moments" is a key part of good leadership.

Jesus was a master at recognizing these teachable moments. A favorite example is found in Mark 10: 42-45. James and John had just come to Jesus and asked if they could each have a special place at his side when he came into His Kingdom. It seems that Jesus was anticipating this moment and used it to call the Twelve together to teach them something that would last throughout their lives: The Kingdom of God is not built upon control or coercion, but upon serving. This teaching was made more memorable because it came out of an actual situation; all three of the synoptic Gospels record both Jesus' words and the context. Contextual teaching comes from shared experiences, not simply listening to principles or information being expounded. Years ago, I remember asking my friend Randeep when he built in time to teach his disciples. He replied that he was teaching them every day, as they lived life together. During our Journeys of Compassion, we begin with specific teaching and training sessions, since the team members come from all over the world and from many different church backgrounds. However, much of the most important teaching happens on the bus or out in the towns and villages as various situations come up. Learning to recognize teachable moments continues to be a growth process for me.

IMITATION

By including the disciples so thoroughly in His life, Jesus facilitated almost endless opportunities for them to watch and learn as He ministered and taught. The Gospels are filled with their eye-witness accounts of what Jesus did, and therefore how he was training them. As recorded in both Matthew and Luke, for a number of months, the disciples watched how Jesus ministered, asking questions and learning from His example. Then came the day when He sent them out on their own to do what they had seen Him do. This may seem both simple and obvious, but it is largely a missing ingredient in our western model.

Modeling and imitation are incredibly effective in the disciple making process. We see this clearly in Luke 9 and 10 where Jesus sends out first the twelve, then the seventy-two. When the seventy-two returned full of joy and eager to tell Him what had happened, Jesus greeted them, saying, "I saw Satan fall like lightning." I believe He said that, not because the seventy-two had been successful in ministry; rather, I think it was about the power of multiplication. When Jesus began His ministry, He came announcing that the Kingdom of Heaven had come; the Kingdom now had a name and a face—one representative. About eighteen months later, He sent out the twelve to do what they had seen Jesus do. Now the Kingdom had thirteen representatives. When, sometime later, the seventy-two returned, the Kingdom now had eighty-five representatives, and Jesus knew that there was no stopping its continued advance through the rapid multiplication of effective ministers.

Another clear example of the power of imitation is found In Mark 5. Jesus followed Jairus, a Jewish leader, to his home because his daughter had just died. Upon arriving, Jesus took Peter, James and John into the dead girl's room where there were a number of mourners. Jesus put them all out of the room before saying to the girl, "Arise". In Acts 9, Peter is summoned to the house of Dorcas, a woman who has died. Just like he saw Jesus do, Peter put everyone out of the room, prayed, then, also as he had seen Jesus do, spoke to Dorcas, "Arise". After all, Jesus had promised, "Whoever believes in Me will also do the works that I do" (Jn 14:12).

There is an immediacy and practicality to this method of discipleship that can't be replicated in a Bible class. As already stated, we need sound instruction, but we also have great need for putting the gospel into practice.

Disciple-making is built upon following, imitating and releasing; this not only leads to multiplication of ministry, but exponential *acceleration*. When people go out with a teacher to watch and then do what they see being done, they are quickly brought into the activity of the Kingdom. If there is one thing that we have learned, it is that Jesus is always on the move, and He moves faster than we thought He would. Hands-on, practical equipping is the fastest way we know to make disciples who follow Jesus.

Our goal in making disciples is to see the Kingdom of God continually advance by multiplying the number of those doing the ministry of Jesus. We want to raise up as many men and women as we can who will build on what they have learned and then go beyond where we have ever been. This is an essential way we measure success in God's Kingdom. Frankly, in my experience of teaching pastors and leaders around the world, this goal is antithetical to much of what they have been trained to do. For many pastors, the church is structured like a pyramid, with the senior pastor at the top. In this traditional structure, there is precious little room for raising up others (especially the younger generation) to do effective ministry. These are not bad leaders; rather, they have been immersed in a bad system, one that copies the ideals and structures of the world. When we can learn to measure our effectiveness by how many others we have released into fruitful ministry, we will see a huge increase in the number, quality and scope of disciples in the church.

Somehow, by the goodness of Jesus, I saw this many years ago. As a result, I have always striven to be specifically raising up younger men and women as disciples who do the works that Jesus called us to. I have four grown sons—and 14 grandchildren! I still remember vividly the day I said to my first born, who was 4 years old, "It's time for you to learn to pray for people. Do you want to come with Daddy to the hospital?" And so, his journey began. Our church had a converted school bus that we used to take food and clothing to the poor in various housing projects. None of my children can remember a time when they didn't go and do that. It became part of their spiritual DNA, and now I watch as they impart this to their children. Now I get to minister with both my children and grandchildren. What a blessing to be with them as they pray for the sick and feed the hungry in poor neighborhoods in our city. Through their practical experience, my grandchildren know that they are ready to follow Jesus into the harvest field right now, and not at some indeterminate later time.

I also have spiritual sons and daughters who have gone with me and my wife to the poor and the sick—both in our city and in countries around the developing world. And as they have come with me, I have watched them grow in confidence, anointing and authority. To my delight, there are several who have surpassed me.

Almost twenty years ago, a young man named Noah came to me and said, "I've been watching you for a while now. I want to be with you when you are ministering so I can learn." From that day on, whenever I was going out to pray for someone in the hospital, when I was taking food to the poor, when I was invited to speak at a church—in each case, I always invited Noah along. Even though he was a young husband and father, he invariably came along. In the beginning, he would watch me. Then, as I watched him, Noah would do what he had seen me do. After each time, on the way home we would talk about what he had noticed, what he had learned. It was a joy to watch Noah grow in confidence, authority and anointing. After some time, when my schedule would not allow me to say yes to various invitations from churches, I would recommend that they invite Noah. I remember a church in London, England contacting me after Noah's visit and telling me what an incredible job he had done in taking them out to do the Gospel. The truth is, after a few years of this kind of modeling discipleship, Noah became more effective on the streets than I ever was. This is successful discipling.

Now, over the past 40+ years of ministry, I have picked up a few things about the power of imitation in forming disciples:

The starting point is to be asking the Lord, "Who are You bringing to me now?". I have asked Him this for at least 30 years. Sometimes His answer comes from existing relationships, but at other times it happens with virtual strangers. Last year while I was conducting a conference in Bulgaria, I asked Jesus if there was someone He was showing me. Almost immediately, He drew my attention to a young couple sitting in the congregation. I spoke very briefly to them after the final session, inviting them to contact me if they ever wanted. I left it at that, because it is important that I never draw anyone to me on the strength of my personality. I only want to be in step with God's plan. Today, Steve and Roni are a true son and daughter to me, with whom I spend significant time each week (it is so good to be in the era of electronic video communication!). I have also flown over to Bulgaria three times this past year to be with them and to model ministry for them. On multiple occasions, they have watched me share the Gospel to groups of people. They have observed how I pray for sick and injured people on the streets, then point these people to the One who healed them. Now, this is what they consistently do.

Sometimes discipleship is extremely practical. I remember having Roni sit on their living room floor with Steve watching as I showed them the best way to baptize people in a shallow pool. Now they do the baptizing. Likewise, they have watched as I introduced new believers to the Lord's Supper and explained its meaning and significance, tying it to the cross, which then opened up a whole other area of teaching. Afterwards, in each case, the three of us would talk about what they had seen and learned. This provides the best opportunity for them to discover what they can now do on their own, and what needs more exposure or teaching. Now, they are continually making disciples among the Roma (gypsy) people, teaching them how to follow Jesus and how to lead others. They have established First Churches and a network is forming. This is the power of modeling and imitation.

Unless unavoidable, I never minister alone. As I write this, I am in Nepal. I have been away in for about six weeks. When I get home next week (and after I have a few days to get over jet lag) I will be going out to the poor in my city. It is really important to me that I don't just do ministry overseas; I need to be about the Father's business (Lu 2:49) at home, too. Those who I am discipling in my home city will minister alongside me, then go do it on their own. After a couple of times, I will ask them to bring one or two along with them. Discipleship is always an opportunity for multiplication. This key principle is found in Paul's final letter:

> *"You should teach people whom you can trust the things you and many others have heard me say. Then they will be able to teach others."*
>
> *(2 Ti 2:2 NCV)*

This passage is not just referring to the sermons or Bible lessons we teach in our small groups; this refers to all aspects of our own walk with the Lord. Through modeling and imitation, those who follow us see first-hand that discipleship is not built on theory; it is practical (just as the Kingdom of God is). For those whose discipleship has been limited to classroom or small group instruction, this is a monumental shift. This puts the "go" back into the Gospel. And remember—disciples make disciples.

Doing ministry with others provides the best forum for instruction. As we saw with Jesus, ministry opens the doors to contextual, situational teaching. It raises questions that are pertinent and practical. I always use the time driving back from ministry to invite questions about what was seen or experienced. These are always the best questions and open the door for the most effective teaching. In this environment of doing ministry, disciples soon see that this is not difficult, and with this realization, fear (sometimes longstanding) melts away. This is one of the great strengths of the imitation model.

My over-arching goal as a leader is to raise up as many men and women as possible who, through imitating me, go beyond where I have ever gone. I want them to be more effective than me in as many aspects of ministry as possible. When I lead teams around the developing world, I always take a disciple with me. They watch me teach the team, preach the Gospel in villages, pray for the sick, teach local pastors and leaders, and provide overall encouragement and direction. And in *all* of these activities, I first model, then have them do the ministry. As the days go by, I purposely decrease my direct involvement so that the disciples can grow in confidence as they discover that they really *do* have spiritual authority and anointing. The result is that there are now a whole group of men and women, a generation younger than me, who are leading Impact Nations teams around the world. Through this kind of discipleship, they can quickly learn what has taken me many years, build upon it, and then go further than me. The unique gifts and personalities that God has given to every person find fulfilment in the midst of discipleship.

While pastoring in Vancouver, I started going downtown to the "flophouses". These were rather terrible hotels run by slumlords with only one bathroom per floor and no cooking facilities. The rooms were occupied by men and women who were often at the end of their rope, just one government check from being put out on the street. I would make some bag lunches, go door to door, and offer to pray for people. After several weeks, one of the single men in our church found out what I was doing every Wednesday morning and asked if he could come along. Before long, he was bringing others. Now we had a team instead of just me. We could make a lot more lunches and we could visit a lot more rooms. I quickly noticed that Mark was more comfortable than I was at just talking and visiting with the people. On our trips home, he shared more and more stories of significant and profound interactions with people. After several months, Mark came to me with news that almost shocked me: He had decided to sell his condominium in a good part of town and move into one of the flophouses. For the next two years or so, Mark lived among the hopeless men and women who lived with drug and alcohol addiction. And what did Mark do for them? He loved them. His room was always open (which in that environment was, itself, a huge gesture of trust). The elements for communion were always on a table. Soft worship music played. Mark's room became a refuge and a place of love, acceptance and hope. He also became an advocate against the injustices suffered by many of the people. Mark followed me into the darkness of the flophouses, learned from me, and then went far beyond where I had ever gone. Imitation is about much more than replication; it is about releasing men and women into greater works.

Imitation is at the heart of Biblical discipleship. It is how the Kingdom of God steadily multiplied in the first century. It is the same today. Remember Randeep—his testimony is that he began his ministry with just he and his wife Anu. Through multiplication by imitation, as of this writing there are now more than 800,000 disciples in northern India.

As I have already stated, when Jesus said, "Follow Me", it was both an *invitation* and *challenge* to go where He was going. It is important that we learn to balance both stretching and encouraging those we are discipling. Jesus did not *point* the way; he *led* the way. A reality that effective leaders have faced for two millennia is that people will not do what we say; they will do what they see us doing. This is actually very good news, because it is by going out and doing what Jesus did that we, and those who are following us, find both the power and the joy of the Gospel. Doing the Gospel is very attractive; it is what we were created for. Therefore, as we follow Jesus into the world around us, men and women who believe that there has to be more will be drawn to us. It isn't ever really us they are attracted to; it is the abundant life of Christ being released in and around us.

> *"You make known to me the path of life; In your presence there is fullness of joy"*
>
> *(Ps 16:11 ESV)*

PUTTING IT INTO PRACTICE

The opportunities to apply what Jesus did in the context of First Church gatherings and of one-on-one discipling are almost endless. I will offer only a few ideas which, hopefully, will launch many more creative applications for all who are reading this book.

We are following the infinitely creative God who never ceases to open up new insights and ways of doing things for all who are hungry for more.

TEACHING

Remember: Disciples make disciples. For most of us, when we think of teaching believers, we picture some kind of classroom or home Bible study setting. But part of making a disciple means teaching them as we live life together. (In Chapter 13 we will look at what to teach a disciple in detail.)

1. The most effective teaching comes from any real-life situations that arise. In order to recognize these, obviously we must spend time with our disciple beyond

structured teaching time. Consider how to facilitate these kinds of opportunities. How do we build in this kind of time into the relationship?

2. In the First Church or small group setting, recognize "teachable moments" that come naturally from the group members as they share what is going on in each of their lives. Teachable moments also arise from more of a "question and answer" format than a monolog approach.

3. Jesus taught in order to confront the heart and *prompt a change* in His listeners. How can we teach in this way rather than teaching Bible passages for the sake of sharing information in a way that may be interesting, but doesn't bring about transformation?

IMITATION

I believe that showing others *how to do* ministry rather than just teaching ideas, is one of the greatest dividing lines in the whole subject of making disciples. If we are going to be making disciples, modeling is undoubtedly one of the most crucial commitments we can make. As a pastor, church planter and leader of a movement with men and women from all over the globe, I watch the power of modeling to activate and empower both individuals, small groups, and entire churches. If we are going to make authentic disciples, I cannot overemphasize the importance of modeling.

Looking at discipling in the context of one-on-one ministry, I offer the following guidelines:

1. Whenever you are going to do ministry (e.g. praying for someone at the hospital or their home; visiting the poor or elderly; praying for people in a neighborhood etc.), *always* take your disciple with you. Always.

2. Beyond spontaneous opportunities that arise, schedule specific times when you can go out together.

3. Begin with the "discipleship loop":

   • Demonstrate the ministry (healing; praying; care for the poor etc.). Have the disciple watch. Discuss what they observed.

   • Have the disciple do the ministry while you watch. Discuss their experience.

   • As the disciple becomes more comfortable, have him or her find someone that they bring along to observe and do ministry with.

Here are some starting ideas for modeling within the context of the First Church or small group gathering:

1. As a group, pick a date for going "outside the walls". Together, decide where and when to go.

2. So that this becomes part of the DNA of the group, agree

on a regularly scheduled date. I recommend going out as a group once every 6 to 8 weeks.

3. Begin with low risk/high success activities. For example: giving out small bags of fruit door to door and then praying a blessing; giving out hot coffee to the homeless; going to a housing project or park in a poor neighborhood and having a simple picnic with hotdogs and cold drinks. After a while, move into going to homes to pray for the sick, or offering "spiritual readings" (prophetic words). The ideas are endless. *What* the group does is less important than simply going out and allowing yourselves to be stretched by the Lord.

4. Finish each outreach with gathering together for a time of sharing what each person's experience has been. It is very important to "celebrate your victories". Rev. 12:11 tells us that we overcome (including our fears and doubts) by the word of our testimony.

5

How Did Jesus Make Disciples?
Part Two

"'Come and see.' They came saw where He was
staying and remained with Him"

John 1:39

When Jesus came up from the waters of His baptism, He heard the Father say: "You are My beloved Son in whom I am well pleased". As Ed Piorek has pointed out, this was the central event for Jesus, for both His life and ministry.[1] Hearing His Father say that Jesus belonged to Him and was loved, brought a deep experience of both identity and security to His life. This was His life-spring; this is what Jesus gave away to everyone. Earlier, I wrote that the two universal needs are security and significance. Belonging is the cradle of security. To be included is essential to our healing and wellbeing.

---

1 Ed Piorek *The Central Event* Anaheim CA: Vineyard International Publishers, 2005

More than fifty years ago, something happened that changed my life. For most of my school years I lived with a strong sense of being somewhat of a social outcast. I had very few friends over the years. I lived as an introvert, expecting to be ignored or excluded. In high school, I was small and fairly uncoordinated and so failed at sports. I dreaded when teams were being picked in gym class because I knew I would be selected last. I lived with the conviction that there wasn't anything I was good at, and that included making friends. I will never forget the day my father came home and announced that we would be moving across the country to a new city. Deep down, I felt that this was my opportunity for a whole new life. But of course, when we moved, I brought my shy and insecure self with me.

In my new classroom, sitting next to me was a teenaged boy who started to invite me to come out for the school choir. Even though I was secretly pleased to be invited, out of my insecurity, I kept turning his invitation down. He persisted and after several weeks, I finally said yes and, although I knew very little about music, I joined. This opened up a whole new world for me. I discovered that I had a lot of music inside me. Quickly, I was singing in various vocal groups. Before long, I was playing three instruments. All these things were in me, but they needed to be discovered. I was finding out who I really was. A shy teenaged boy grew into a confident young man who had a sense of his true identity. Just as importantly, I was invited into a group of friendly, accepting teens who valued and affirmed one another. For the first time, I knew I was accepted; even deeper, I knew that I belonged. Again, belonging is the cradle of security. That is why belonging is at the core of the Gospel.

INCLUSION

The third way that Jesus made disciples was through inclusion. He very intentionally lived His life with others. This wasn't some of the time; this was *how* Jesus lived His life every day. Wherever He went, Jesus continuously made room in His life and in His heart for people. To everyone—including the sick, the marginalized, the despised, the morally defeated—to all of them Jesus lived His life with His arms opened wide, expressing and demonstrating the power of His unconditional love, acceptance and forgiveness. Everything about Him said, "You come too! Of course, you're included!"

Jesus lived with no boundaries. He didn't see the world dualistically, with everyone either being "us" or "them". One day, the disciples came to Jesus with a complaint that was the result of their "in or out" worldview.

> *"Teacher, we saw someone using Your name to force demons out of a person. We told him to stop, because he does not belong to our group."*
>
> *But Jesus said, "Don't stop him, because anyone who uses My name to do powerful things will not easily say evil things about me. Whoever is not against us is with us."*
>
> *(Mk 9:38-40 NCV)*

Because of Jesus' radical inclusiveness, He welcomed men and women from very different backgrounds and social status.

Fishermen, employees of the Romans, zealots committed to the overthrow of these same Romans, villagers, city people—everyone was invited. He reached across ethnic barriers to Canaanite and Samaritan women, and to those suffering in the largely Gentile region of the Decapolis. In an age of strong gender-based boundaries, He reached out to, and included, women. Sometimes the place of women in Jesus' life and ministry is underappreciated. Besides His mother, many other women were part of Jesus' band of disciples. A number are specifically named, including Mary Magdalene, Joanna, Susanna, and Martha and Mary, the sisters of Lazarus. In the hills of rural Galilee, Jesus said,

> *"Come unto Me all who are heavy-laden and I will give you rest."*
> *(Mt 11:28 CSB)*

At the Temple in Jerusalem in the midst of a Jewish festival, Jesus cried out in a loud voice,

> *"If anyone is thirsty let him come to Me and drink"*
> *(Jn 7:37 CSB)*

Jesus lived the most inclusive life that was ever lived; this came from His own deep experience of belonging and acceptance. This was not a one-time event that took place at His baptism. It is my conviction that when He rose to pray each morning, usually in a secluded place (Mk 1:35), Jesus experienced the power of the Father's words: "You are My beloved Son; in You I am well pleased". What He continually received is what He continually gave away. This unconditional inclusiveness and acceptance healed wounded lives, like the woman at the well (Jn 4) who out of her encounter with Him, ran to the very town that had always rejected her and told them about this Jesus who knew everything about her, yet accepted her. Notice that this Samaritan woman was the first evangelist in the Bible! I am always moved by the account of the prostitute in Luke 7 who out of her desperation, and in spite of her shame, breaks into a dinner and weeps at the feet of Jesus. He never pushes her away or tells her to get control of herself; instead Jesus receives this woman in all of her brokenness and gives her the gift of forgiveness and acceptance. Tradition tells us that this woman was Mary Magdalene, whose life was so transformed by Jesus' inclusion that she came to be known as "the apostle to the apostles.".

> Perhaps the most powerful way that Jesus went about the re-forming of lives was by His inclusive life. More than anyone, He lived the gift of welcome.

Jean Vanier, the founder of the L'Arche movment, has described living inclusively as the "gift of welcome".[2] The gift of welcome is the decision to make room in our lives, (including our schedules and priorities) and our hearts, where we choose to embrace the best in others and ourselves. The choice to live an inclusive life necessitates being intentionally available to others. We will look at this more closely later when we examine what Biblical hospitality really means.

---

2   Jean Vanier, *Community and Growth* (Paulist Press 1989) p. 245ff

Perhaps the most powerful way that Jesus went about the re-forming of lives—which is at the heart of disciple-making—was by His inclusive life. More than anyone, He lived the gift of welcome: in His words, actions, and priorities (for example, ministering to others even when He was exhausted). Those around Him instinctively felt safe and valued; there was depth to His welcome that was highly impacting. Jesus knew the power of a shared life—eating, sleeping, traveling, and talking. This was the environment of real disciple-making. By living inclusively, by welcoming others into His life, Jesus provided the ideal environment for disciple-making. In the growing intimacy of true community, each disciple experienced a safe place where he could ask questions, where each one could learn from the others. So much of what Jesus taught them was really "caught"; it was imparted to the disciples as they watched and learned from simply being with Jesus. Every day provided multiple opportunities to grow. It was in the slow, steady process of learning to live together that unbreakable bonds were formed which would unite these men and women in the midst of great persecution, of incredibly difficult travel around the Roman world, and even of martyrdom. As the disciples lived each day with Jesus—*and with one another*—they were slowly becoming who they were really created to be. Together, they were discovering their authority, their anointing—and their weaknesses and failings. Being with Jesus everyday was both exposing and transforming them.

From the day of Pentecost, the disciples were demonstrating and establishing what they had learned and experienced for over three years with Jesus: *family*. As the days became weeks, months and years, their relationship with Jesus and one another grew into something so powerful that it would influence the rest of their lives. Jesus helped them to recognize this new paradigm that went far beyond religious service or faithfulness to a cause. On His final evening with the disciples, He helped them to identify that the journey they had been on with Him was not built upon the foundation of successful ministry, but upon the discovery of a whole new kind of family.

> *I no longer call you servants, because a servant does not know his master's business. Instead, I have called you friends, for everything that I learned from my Father I have made known to you.*
>
> *(Jn 15:15 NIV)*

THE CHALLENGE

To read in the Gospels the accounts of the early church, is to see that every aspect of life was shared: their time, resources, where they slept and ate, and their activities. It is interesting that the first place Jesus took the disciples in John's Gospel was not to the synagogue or to do ministry; instead, He took them to a party, a wedding ceremony. Jesus did nothing without purpose. In this first outing, He was demonstrating that *all* of life is sacred and to be shared. Have you ever noticed how many exchanges with Jesus took place while they ate? In all cultures there is nothing more effective in building family than sharing meals together. After all, much of the dynamic of family life happens around the dinner table. When our four sons lived at home, the highlight of every day was the exchange of news, victories and struggles that were freely shared as we ate together. This shared life that the disciples experienced with Jesus is what they passed on from the first day of the early church.

The life that Jesus modeled presents us with at least two challenges: first, to disciple another person in this way opens us up to our own vulnerabilities. If our relationship is largely based upon me preaching a sermon on Sunday, or getting together for a scheduled mentoring meeting, I am in control of the situation and environment. However, a shared, inclusive life is intrinsically less secure. It requires authenticity and transparency. It means a willingness to be seen in all situations. As I open up my life to those I am discipling, quickly they see that I am not perfect, or even close to it. Now, my own failures become some of the teachable moments. Jesus said that the way to real life was to die to ourselves (Jn 12:24). As a leader, living a truly inclusive life makes these words (sometimes painfully) real. Yet if we die to ourselves, we find true life in Him, and in His family.

Secondly, in the West, our lives are largely agenda-driven. Most hours of the day are filled with appointments, meetings and various commitments. Wherever I go in the developing world where the church is experiencing explosive growth, I am always very aware of how much less structured their time is. Plans are held very loosely; what we would often feel is an interruption, they usually see as an interesting new variation that the Holy Spirit is presenting. I don't know anyone in India or Africa who pulls out his or her phone to see when the next appointment is. This different approach to time has significant implications. Deep, authentic relationship is not possible without fellowship. Fellowship requires time together. It is not a feeling; it is the product of determining to prioritize living our lives corporately.

We live in a time in the West where there is much talk about the importance of quality time. However, all sociological studies show that this is a myth. What is required is *quantity* time.[3] There is no indication anywhere in the Gospels that Jesus limited His time with His disciples. For over three years, they were formed in the midst of daily life with Jesus. If we continue to embrace our modern, highly scheduled lifestyles, how can we move toward the inclusive discipleship of Jesus? The only answer is to face the need for change—and real change always costs us. To leave our preferred and familiar ways of doing things is discomforting. The single most repeated saying of Jesus is: "Whoever seeks to save his life will lose it, but whoever loses his life for My sake, will find it." This is the great challenge—to give up living as we have always known it and embrace living in a very different way, built on different values and priorities. Yet, Jesus' words also offer a promise: to enter into a whole new kind of life, marked by relational abundance and joy. Will we exchange the known for the unknown? Will we follow Jesus into a radically inclusive and welcoming life, knowing that it will likely cost us our privacy, preferences, and comfort—yet trusting that He is leading us into what we have, deep down, always hoped for?

---

3   https://www.imom.com/time-quality-time-quantity-time/#.XHdzQy2B-0Wo; https://www.patrickwanis.com/the-quality-time-myth-its-quantity-time-that-matters/

I am on a journey with this and I have a long way to go. It means moving beyond making scheduled appointments with those I am pastoring. Instead, I am learning to be available whenever they need or want to talk. This journey means being less bound by my planned agenda. This has been a real challenge for me, since I am a classic Type A personality who for years has set daily goals. I am gradually learning to be more flexible and free with my time, trusting that the Lord really *does* know better than I do how my day should be spent. But deeper than that, I am on a journey to give up my preference for an ample amount of private time. Although I have made it a habit for years to take people out with me to minister, now I am discovering the deep and long-term value of spending "quantity time" together, without any agenda, knowing that it is the environment of unstructured times—of simply doing life together—where the gold of discipleship is found.

PUTTING IT INTO PRACTICE

The opportunities to apply what Jesus did in the context of First Church gatherings and in one-on-one discipling are almost endless. I will offer only a few ideas which, hopefully, will launch many more creative applications for all who are reading this book.

We are following an infinitely creative God who never ceases to open up new insights and ways of doing things for all who are hungry for more.

Living inclusively, where we make room for others in our

hearts and lives, is both a choice and a journey, challenging our priorities and preferences. This will not come naturally. It will take a determined effort to live and feel differently, both individually and as a First Church or small group.

1. Since most discipling comes from the spontaneous teachable moments, make the deliberate choice to include one or more people in your life. This will mean sharing meals, having an "open door" policy where the disciple knows he or she is always welcome to come by. My children don't have to make an appointment; they are always welcome. This is family.

2. You might consider inviting a disciple to live with your family. This has been our pattern for almost 35 years. Authentic discipling happens in open, familial environments.

3. An important component of First Church is living beyond the boundaries of a set meeting time and place. So, start spending more time together: games nights, picnics, going out for supper together, eat in one another's homes outside of the regular gathering. It doesn't have to be the whole First Church (although that is great, too); whenever any of the group are together, that's the First Church. How much more attractive to invite a new friend to come and meet your other friends (family) than to invite them to a meeting. Live this way, and watch "the Lord add daily to your number".

6

A Turning Point

"Behold, I make all things new."

Rev. 21:5

Within days of walking into a church as a new believer over forty years ago, I became a member of a small group. We called them house fellowship groups back then. From the beginning, I enjoyed the gatherings. I remember that we met in a house every Wednesday evening. It was a place where I could make Christian friends (because I had never had any before), where I could learn the simple choruses we sang in those days, where I could learn about the Bible, and where we prayed for each other.

Since then, I have learned a lot about small groups; in fact, in the 90's I was responsible for teaching about them in the denomination where I was a member. So, I have lots (I mean, *lots*) of books about small groups. I know about cell groups, G-12 groups, affinity groups, connect groups, home groups, life groups and…well, you get the idea. So why am I writing about First Churches? Aren't there enough books out there on various forms of Christian small groups? Yes, there are. But what I am sharing with you is something fundamentally different.

Perhaps the best way to understand this difference is to point out what a First Church is *not*. From the beginning, I want to be clear: I am not critical of small groups; I see that they can have an important role in connecting and caring for the church. I also understand that there are many First Church principles that, when applied to small groups, can help them to flourish with new vitality and vision (and people!).

Whatever they are called (life groups, care groups, home groups etc.), almost all of them have some of the same characteristics. The groups usually meet in someone's home, often the leader's house. The meeting time is set for the same time and place each week. When it is time for the leader to call the meeting together, if someone can play a guitar or piano, the gathering usually starts with three or four songs that the members know, often followed by the host leader sharing some announcements. These may be directly related to the group (like a need that a member has) or about activities going on at the church. Typically, this is followed by a Bible study. These tend to happen in a few ways: the leader takes the group through a study that he or she has prepared; or there is a study based on a particular book that the group is going through; or it is a study prepared by the church staff based upon the sermon that was preached on the previous Sunday. This is often followed by prayer: either the members break into groups of two or three to pray for one another, or needs are expressed around the circle and then everyone is invited to pray. The meeting finishes with refreshments. This typical small group model is in most ways a miniature version of the Sunday morning service. This is what people have experienced each Sunday, and so it makes sense that it is the model that they copy.

In his seminal book, *How Churches Grow*, Donald McGavran recognized that churches gravitate to one of two poles: nurture and mission. Nurture is about caring for the members, creating a safe and stable environment for believers. Mission is about reaching outside of the church to connect with those who don't know Christ. McGavran also noted that years of careful research revealed that the nurture pull is *nine times stronger* that the pull toward mission. After years of leading and overseeing church small groups, I have seen this to be unwaveringly true. The differences between small groups and First Churches clearly illustrate this polarity.

I have been present for the start of more small groups than I can count. Usually the leader begins on the first night by going around the circle and asking people why they have come and what they are hoping to see in this group. With remarkable consistency, the response is the same: we are here to build relationships, to pray together and to read the Bible together. Typically, one or two people will state that they would like the group to do some outreach. The others nod in approval, knowing that evangelism is a good value to have. However, meaningful outreach almost never happens. When it is brought up, usually after two or three months, the majority expresses their doubt that it is time yet. "We need more time to bond. We have developed such a great group here, we don't want that dynamic to change. We haven't had any training on how to do outreach," etc. Most small groups in the West do not grow, and if they do, the growth comes from other believers (often from the Sunday gathering). In the western church, small groups are a place for Christians to gather. This isn't bad, but it is true.

Again, there is nothing wrong with this model; every church that I planted was built on small groups. They provide a great training ground for the small group leader and they are a good way to keep members connected beyond the Sunday meeting. However, this model has some significant limitations, especially related to the issue of actually making disciples. No matter what they are called, what do you notice about the small group outline that we presented (besides the fact that most of you immediately recognize it)? That's right. It is mini-church. It is church on Sunday done again on Wednesday in someone's home.

A DIFFERENT KIND OF CHURCH MEETING

Here is an excerpt from <u>The Journey</u>, which describes my first encounter with a house church. The impact of that first exposure has never left me.

> For more than 30 years, I have been fascinated by the early church. During its first three centuries, through persecution, slander and rejection, the church grew

at an unprecedented rate without the benefit of public gatherings or buildings. For many years, my reading has led me to an interest in the house church movement in China and India. A number of years ago, I heard about Victor Choudhrie and a movement that began in his home in the early 1990's. This movement now includes many millions of people all over India. The numbers are staggering: for each of the past three years they have celebrated Pentecost Sunday by baptizing one million new believers in towns and villages all over the nation. Hundreds of new house churches are being added every day.

In 2013, I flew halfway around the world to see for myself what was happening. In a three-week span, I traveled over 2,500 kilometers while in India, visiting house churches in isolated villages, farms, city slums and modern middle-class neighborhoods. With impeccable timing, I was in India during the most severe heat wave in forty years; I remember one day was 51°C/124°F. Yet even this didn't stop people from crowding into small rooms with little or no ventilation. God was moving powerfully, and no one wanted to miss out.

My friend Anuroop and I drove into a remote, rural area populated by the Banjara people. The Romany people (sometimes referred to as gypsies) originated from this region and descended from the Banjaras. Many centuries ago some of them emigrated to Persia and on to what is now Eastern Europe. The Banjaras are an isolated, poor tribal people, largely ignored by the surrounding communities. We stayed overnight at a friend's home; the next morning people began to arrive from all over. After some time, there were 46 men, women and children packed into the small house. I was about to witness a new and totally different kind of home gathering.

No one called the meeting to order, or even asked if someone had a scripture or prayer. Instead, the Holy Spirit led. Someone began singing and others joined in. Then another person began a song that was picked up by all. Someone began to pray, then a scripture was read, then another song. For 2½ hours, there was a continual flow of testimonies, songs, prayers, scriptures and teaching—and all of this happening with no one directing in any way.

At one point, a young girl of about 13 years of age read a passage from 1 Samuel, then began to share with the church what the Lord had spoken to her through this passage. It was a remarkably deep teaching, full of revelation. Another person told an original parable about a factory manager and his workers. A woman testified that earlier in the week, while in prayer, the Holy Spirit told her that a certain man in the village had died. She was directed to go to his house and, rather than praying for the man, she was to preach the Gospel over his corpse. She did exactly that. The man suddenly began to breathe and then sat up. I was astounded, yet all around me there seemed to be no surprise, just thanksgiving. Someone else shared that she had had a wonderful week, leading 22 of her neighbors to Christ. Then she baptized them all at her home. Twenty-two neighbors in one week. Another woman told of going to a home where a woman had died. She laid hands on her and prayed; Jesus brought the woman back from the dead. Once again, there was no surprise expressed among the church members, only thankfulness and joy.

New believers shared their stories of recently coming to Christ and of how excited they were to tell all their neighbors about what Jesus had done. Many testified of meeting the Lord through the kindness of a stranger who later became a brother or sister. In this incredible atmosphere of faith, love and victory, many of those visiting for the first time also gave their lives to Jesus.

> The time flew by and I didn't want this gathering to ever end. No wonder the house churches keep multiplying all over the nation. Who wouldn't want to be in the midst of this?

Finally, the host in this small Banjara village spoke. For the whole time he had been simply watching and enjoying what the Lord was doing. He said to those gathered, "Once again, the Lord has richly blessed us. This has been a wonderful time. It is near the end of the month and I know that you have all been asking the

Holy Spirit about how many disciples (new believers) you should be asking Him for over the next month. Let's take a few minutes and each one can tell what He has said to you." Without hesitation, all the believers spoke out a specific number. The lowest I heard that morning was five; the highest I remember was forty. One woman began to weep loudly. She told us that earlier in the year, she had asked the Lord for 300 new disciples this year. She had already surpassed that goal and it was only May. When she prayed, the Holy Spirit told her, "Daughter, why don't you ask me for 3,000?" It was this answer that had brought her to tears. She was convinced that the Lord would give these people to her.

Afterward, I thought of what the Apostle Paul told the Corinthians: when the church gathers, each one has something to contribute (1 Cor. 14:26). As each person stepped out and shared, it was as though the Lord was weaving a tapestry that was different every time they gathered, but always made from the mutual love, joy and faith that each individual added. This is what I saw, and it was thrilling. The time flew by and I didn't want this gathering to ever end. No wonder the house churches keep multiplying all over the nation. Who wouldn't want to be in the midst of this?

This was my first Indian house church experience and it has had a profound impact on me. Later, I saw this repeated again and again as I traveled around India for the next three weeks. Each gathering was unique, but what tied them together was a great excitement and appreciation for what the Lord was doing, and a hunger among all the participants to continually reach their friends and neighbors with the amazing story of the Gospel.

At each gathering, time seemed to fly by; I felt like I had stepped into the Book of Acts—and it was a great place to be. As a North American pastor, I had for years studied techniques, strategies and programs designed to help the church grow. But what I saw in India was organic; it had so much life that it couldn't help but grow. Just like the early church.[1]

It is obvious that the First Church and small group model differ, but the differences go well beyond style or practice. These models are rooted in profoundly different values and motivations, leading to very different results. While the First Church movement, when practiced with the values that we will later describe, is exploding in various parts of the world, small group membership is at best plateaued and is more likely in numeric decline, reflecting the steady decline in church membership in the West over the past forty years.

On more than one occasion, Jesus told us to look at the fruit of

---

1 Steve Stewart, *The Journey* (Albuquerque: Impact Nations Publishing, 2015) p. 161.

something. I am writing this book and sharing this story with believers all over the world because the fruit is so exciting. Not only is the growth of First Churches explosive, they are a wineskin that is an ideal vehicle for effective disciple-making. Yet, I come back to the Great Commission: Jesus said to make disciples; He never told us to make First Churches. Whether we adopt the First Church model fully or not, we can glean from the powerful principles of disciple-making that it presents. In fact, most of the First Church principles that I will share in the coming chapters are fully applicable to the wide variety of small groups that are common throughout the western Christian church.

In this next section, we will look at the underlying principles and practices that I first saw evidenced in India. Since then, I have participated in countless First Church gatherings in different countries and entered into their corporate life. First Churches are not another kind of gathering; they are the living out of what the early church discovered after the Day of Pentecost. First Churches are *people—family*—not gatherings. It is this that makes them so supernaturally missional. It is because First Churches are so attractive. They reflect the beautiful Gospel, life as God always intended it to be.

You have picked up this book because you believe that there has to be more, there has to be a better way. This is a longing that the Holy Spirit has put into you as His gift to you. Embrace that longing and get ready for a new adventure.

7

The Early Church: How it all began

*"Don't you realize that all of you together
are the temple of God and that the Spirit of
God lives in you?"*

1 Corinthians 3:16

The desire to draw upon the example of the early church is one of the great motivators among First Church movements. While any objective reading of the New Testament letters will quickly reveal that the early church was no spiritual utopia, it does serve as the best starting point for understanding many of the values of the First Church movement. The first century church was the church in its original form, but not everything can or should be copied in our day; cultural assumptions and practices change. Who, for example, would want to return to slavery or to keeping women quiet when the church gathers? However, the values and ethos of the early church provide us with a template to both build and evaluate how we are practicing church in our day.

The church was born on Pentecost, and Luke provides us with its earliest description.

All the believers devoted themselves to the apostles' teaching, and to fellowship, and to sharing in meals (including the Lord's Supper), and to prayer.

A deep sense of awe came over them all, and the apostles performed many miraculous signs and wonders. And all the believers met together in one place and shared everything they had.

They sold their property and possessions and shared the money with those in need. They worshiped together at the Temple each day, met in homes for the Lord's Supper, and shared their meals with great joy and generosity— all the while praising God and enjoying the goodwill of all the people. And each day the Lord added to their fellowship those who were being saved.

(Acts 2:42-47 NLT)

Countless books have been written about this first church; an in-depth study goes beyond the scope of this book. However, there are some key characteristics that served as building blocks for the church, that it preserved over the first three hundred years. Luke summarizes these:

- A focus on the apostles' teaching
- Time spent together
- Eating their meals together

- Prayer
- Frequent gathering of all the believers
- Miraculous signs
- Material care for those in need

Reading through the rest of the New Testament reveals that the early church never deviated from these core practices.

In an era where it was difficult (sometimes impossible) for the church to meet publicly, the church grew at an unprecedented rate. Remember that from the beginning, "the Lord added daily to their number". How did this happen without evangelistic campaigns and outreaches? Among the many factors, five stand out: *community; a counter-cultural identity; a unique lifestyle; worship and prayer; and the presence of the Lord in their meeting.*

COMMUNITY

The community of the first century church was primarily centered around the house. It was in the house of John Mark's mother where the 120 waited together for ten days after Jesus' ascension. The Holy Spirit first fell upon believers in a house. Throughout the New Testament, the house was always the primary location for the church. Four times in his letters, Paul specifically addresses "the church that meets in (Priscilla and Aquila; Stephanas; Nympha etc.) house". The Thessalonian church met in Jason's house (Acts 17:5); the first house church in Corinth was at the home of Titius Justus (Act 18:7); in Caesarea, the church met in Philip's home (Acts 21:8); in

Philippi the church met in Lydia's home, and also the house of the jailer (Acts 16).

In all cultures, the home is the best environment for building and sustaining a strong sense of community. We see this all over the world; where authentic community is being experienced, people move freely from house to house. The atmosphere of a welcoming home helps people to connect with others more meaningfully, providing a relaxed and informal environment. This in turn encourages trust and openness. The Apostle John admonished the early church to "walk in the light" with one another. Throughout the New Testament there is a call for believers to live with transparency. This can only happen where community is lived out with honesty and authenticity.

Coming together was not one aspect of their busy lives—it *was* their lives. This total re-alignment of their priorities, affecting schedule, activities and friendships, was part of the great appeal of the early church.

In the early days, the church in Jerusalem met primarily in two ways: smaller gatherings in homes and much larger assemblies at Solomon's portico, a covered area adjacent to the courtyard of the Temple. Luke writes that there were at least three thousand believers, and therefore, a large place for corporate gatherings was needed. But the center of their corporate life was lived out in First Churches and the nucleus of these First Churches was the household, the family unit where the church met.

"The household was much broader than the family in modern Western societies, including not only immediate relatives but also slaves, freedmen, hired workers, and sometimes tenants and partners in trade or craft."[1]

Two things stand out about the First Churches: First, they were comprised of people who were naturally connected through their daily activities in society; the early church grew through the relational networks that were formed at work, in the neighborhood, and through common interests. Later, we will see how this approach is being practiced with great fruitfulness today. Second, First Churches were built upon a strong sense of family that transcended blood relations. In addressing the various churches, Paul speaks to them as "brothers and sisters" and "beloved". The household was central to the lives of the First Church members.

The first century church met very frequently, often daily. Assembling together was at the center of their lives. With our modern Western worldview, this may be hard for us to really grasp. If someone says, "house church, or small group or life group", we immediately think of a specific time and place to gather. However, whenever and wherever the church came together, it was a family, not a meeting. And as with most families, the early church gathered much more spontaneously than we typically experience. Coming together was not one aspect of their busy lives—it *was* their lives. This total re-alignment of their priorities, affecting schedule, activities and

---

1 Wayne Meeks, *The First Urban Christians* (New Haven: Yale University Press, 1983), 75

friendships, was part of the great appeal of the early church. Following Christ in community was something worth giving up everything else for and was remarkably attractive to all those who were looking for a great purpose. Michael Green in his classic book, *Evangelism in the Early Church*, saw this new kind of community as the clearest expression of the Gospel.

> "[L]ife together is the Gospel itself expressed in corporate form. Christian community is the shape the Gospel takes when translated into relational terms."[2]

This totally new kind of community *was* the truest expression of the Body of Christ on the earth.

Eating together was at the center of their gatherings. Twice in the Acts 2 passage, Luke emphasizes that, daily, the church shared meals together; in fact, this was the one great constant in their corporate life. For all the believers, the high point of the week was a very special meal: the *agape meal*. It was the central event of their worship practice. The agape meal was where everyone gathered around the table (or tables) and simply shared life—what happened that day; what the Lord had revealed to them that day; what opportunities had opened up for prayer with someone. It included remembering the Cross and Resurrection through the sharing of the bread and the cup. Historians tell us that before the meal, there was a time of blessing; after the meal there was spontaneous worship where each member was encouraged to share a scripture or song.

---

2 Michael Green, *Evangelism in the Early Church* (Wm. B. Eerdmans Pub., 2003) p.42

Recently, I was in Amritsar, India, where the Golden Temple, the most holy site for the Sikh faith, is located. I had been there before, but I had never gone into where the meals are served. Because hospitality and care for the poor are such foundational tenets of the Sikh faith, no one is ever denied a meal, no matter their religion. In fact, over 75,000 people are fed every day at the Golden Temple. I wanted to see this for myself, so I went in with Randeep, my son and some other friends. I was struck by the care and attention we received, as each server took time to look me in the eyes and smile. Given the thousands who were being fed, this greatly impacted me. This may surprise you, but I felt the Lord's presence in a very real way. I think it is because, wherever we are moving in His rhythm of mercy, love and grace—whether we know it or not—He is there. While we ate, Randeep said something profound: "If we eat together, nobody is poor." This is another reason why the agape meal was so precious to the early church. It was a regular, tangible expression of the Gospel's mandate to share what we have. (Lu 3:11) A shared meal reminds us that in this new community, there are no economic, social or racial distinctions.

COUNTER-CULTURAL

Part of the significance of the agape meal was that it crossed social and economic lines. The believers pooled their resources in order to meet individual needs within the church. This was as radical then as it would be today. The early church diligently sought to obey the words of Jesus, including His admonition to avoid storing up treasures on earth (Mt 6:19). This was unheard of in the Roman world.

And all the believers met together in one place and shared everything they had. They sold their property and possessions and shared the money with those in need.

(Acts 2:44-45 NLT)

All the believers were united in heart and mind. And they felt that what they owned was not their own, so they shared everything they had.

(Acts 4:32 NLT)

The central event of the early church, the agape meal, was a powerful mark of its distinctly counter-cultural identity. The believers came together as equals; their bond was love, and the agape meal reflected their transformed relationships. Groups that formerly were separated by ethnicity or economics now sat down together at a family meal. Their refusal to separate from each other contributed to the mistrust that many outsiders felt toward the early Christians. "The Christians were creating an alternative community that had nonconformist approaches to common social problems and that imparted to its participants a powerful sense of individual and group identity. This had immense formative power."[3]

The church lived by a different standard from that of the society around it. While the individual's life in the Roman Empire was not highly valued—unwanted babies were regularly left to die; unwanted wives were summarily discarded; slaves were beaten to death—the early church valued life at every level. The early

3 Alan Kreider, *The Patient Ferment of the Early Church* (Grand Rapids: Baker Publishing Group, 2016) 60.

church was profoundly counter-cultural: marriage was sacred; the church would rescue abandoned children; during times of plague, it was only the Christians who would care for the sick, often at the cost of their own lives. As the early church father, Origen wrote, "The churches were another sort of country, created by the Logos of God."

There was a cost to becoming a follower of Christ. Friends and family ties were broken; employment was lost; believers were often ostracized by their neighbors. At various times, there was persecution by the state that, in extreme cases, led to martyrdom. "When people become Christians, they were converted to marginality."[4]

A UNIQUE LIFESTYLE

The manner in which the early church lived out its faith in Christ was like a lightning rod in the ancient world. Many Romans were threatened and angered by what they saw, but others were powerfully drawn to what was known as "the Way". It was not the Christians' worship or beliefs that confronted and attracted people; it was how they lived. "[T]he outsiders looked at the Christians and saw them energetically feeding poor people and burying them, caring for boys and girls who lacked property and parents, and being attentive to aged slaves and prisoners."[5] As has been true throughout history, it is not the words of

---

4 Wolfgang Simson, *Houses That Change the World* (Authentic Pub, 2000) 46

5 Alan Kreider, *The Patient Ferment of the Early Church* (Grand Rapids: Baker Publishing Group, 2016) 61

Christians that matter so much; rather, it is the demonstration of their commitment to those words.

Tertullian, an early church father in North Africa (155-240AD) famously recorded what the citizens had to say about the Christians: "Look! How they love one another." This reflects what Jesus told His disciples: *"By this everyone will know that you are my disciples, if you have love for one another." (Jn 13:35).* There was a purposefulness, even an intensity to their common life. Justin Martyr, another early church father, wrote, "We are constantly together." Because the early church wasn't a meeting, but a family, it was natural for them to be together daily. And like any family it was completely heterogeneous— men, women, boys, girls, grandparents and children all together in community. This was a huge distinctive in the Roman world.

It is important to note that living as a community did not necessarily mean everyone lived under one roof. The church was born in Jerusalem during the festival of Pentecost. Luke records that 3,000 new believers were added to the church in a single day. This created an interesting challenge for the apostles. During the festival, the population of the city mushroomed to nearly ten times its normal size, as Jews from all over the Empire came to Jerusalem to celebrate Pentecost. This is apparent in the crowd's response to the Holy Spirit falling upon the 120:

How is it that we hear, each of us, in our own native language Parthians, Medes, Elamites; those who live in Mesopotamia, in Judea and Cappadocia, Pontus and Asia Phrygia and Pamphylia, Egypt and the parts of

Libya near Cyrene; visitors from Rome, both Jews and proselytes, Cretans and Arabs—we hear them speaking in our own languages the magnificent acts of God."

(Acts 2:8-11 CSB)

It is likely that of those 3,000 new believers, perhaps 2,500 of them were from out of town; given the description of church life in Acts 3 and 4, it is unlikely that many of them went home. They needed a place to live, at least in the short term, and the best solution was to sleep and eat in the homes of the local believers. This was not usually a permanent solution, but transitional until more housing could be found. However, even after this happened, the believers still lived as a community, every day sharing meals, praying, worshiping and simply living an incredibly rich life together that caught the attention, and often attracted, their neighbors.

Jesus told his followers that they were to be a "city on a hill" and as such, not to hide their light, but let it shine. From multiple early sources—Christian, Roman and Jewish—we know that one of the great distinguishing marks of the church's counter-cultural lifestyle was its care for the poor and the vulnerable. In fact, they were passionate about it. One of the early church fathers, Ignatius, wrote that if the church is not marked by caring for the poor, the oppressed and the hungry, then it is guilty of heresy.[6] By the second century, only those new believers who committed to care for the widow, the orphan and the sick were permitted to be baptized.

---

6   Shane. Claiborne, *The Irresistible Revolution* (Grand Rapids: Zondervan, 332.

It is estimated that about 65% of people in the Roman world lived below the poverty line. This was the economic environment in which the early church not only survived; it flourished. How could this happen? First, their shared life was radically holistic where almost every aspect of their lives was shared. The early church's values and lifestyle were, in many ways, far removed from what we experience today. A literal reading of Hebrews 13:16 is almost shocking to our modern worldview:

> *"And do not neglect beneficence and communal ownership, for with such sacrifices God is delighted."*[7]

This passage can easily conjure up words like "socialism" in the minds of contemporary Christians; nevertheless, this is what the scriptures actually say. If we look at the New Testament honestly and without filters, we are constantly confronted with the gulf that separates many of the values and practices of the early and 21st century church. Tertullian records that,

> At regular intervals, most members, according to their ability, brought donations for the church's common fund that the community's leaders could put at the disposal of the needy members."[8]

Secondly, it was understood that becoming a follower of Christ meant downward mobility. To become part of this counter-

---

7 David Bentley Hart, *The New Testament* (New Haven: Yale University Press, 2017), 454

8 Alan Kreider, *The Patient Ferment of the Early Church* (Grand Rapids: Baker Publishing Group, 2016) 115

cultural family of believers meant intentionally embracing a simpler life. Disciples found satisfaction and even joy in living with just the essentials. In this way, the early church broke free from the almost universal pull toward more possessions, more finances and more prestige.

The early church's care was not limited to its own members. From the beginning, believers helped needy outsiders. One of history's great ironies is that the same society that rejected, mistrusted and mocked the Christians, at the same time was amazed by their care for the destitute, abandoned and sick among Roman population. Clearly, the early church took the words of Jesus in Mt 25 seriously: they openly fed the hungry, clothed the naked, visited prisoners, and took in strangers.

The fourth century historian and bishop, Eusebius, wrote about the way in which the Christians took care of those suffering from plague in his city. He recorded that, because of their compassion in the midst of the plague, the Christians' "deeds were on everyone's lips, and they glorified the God of the Christians."[9]

WORSHIP AND PRAYER IN THE EARLY CHURCH

When the church gathered in an ever-increasing number of homes around towns and cities, what exactly took place? In Jerusalem it seems that much of the teaching (upon which our

---

9   https://biblemesh.com/blog/the-compassion-of-early-christians

modern evangelical services are largely based) took place at the central gathering at Solomon's Portico. What happened in the homes was very organic and interactive. No two gatherings would be the same; however, there were some common features to the church meeting in the home.

For a number of years, the church met daily. For many of us with our modern worldview and lifestyle, this seems hard to grasp. But for these new believers, the church was not a time or place to meet; it was a family. More than that, it was the central relational unit in each of their lives. Just as many of us as children and teens came home every afternoon or early evening to share a meal with our family, likewise, this was automatic for the early church. And the central event of the gathering was the agape meal. As described earlier, it was a literal meal around a table with a wonderful blend of informality and intimacy. Key elements of this meal were worship and scripture reading that all pointed to the climax of the meal, the Lord's Supper. Here, the bread and wine were shared in remembrance of Christ and as an expression of their covenant commitment to each other.

THE PRESENCE OF THE LORD

Another key component of the early church gathering was exercising spiritual gifts. Paul addresses this issue in great depth in his letter to the church in Corinth (see chapters 12-14) where he delineates a large number of specific spiritual gifts that he encourages the believers to practice in their gatherings. A key to understanding what took place in the early house churches is found in Paul's letter to the Corinthians:

So, brothers and sisters, what should you do? When you meet together, one person has a song, and another has a teaching. Another has a new truth from God. Another speaks in a different language, and another person interprets that language. The purpose of all these things should be to help the church grow strong.

(1 Cor 14:26 NCV)

Two things seem clear from this passage: when the church gathered, *each one* was an active participant. There was no clergy/laity divide. Each person expected to be used by the Lord to teach the others. Secondly, each gathering was totally unique, the Holy Spirit moving and speaking with great variety of expression. Every gathering was an exciting new experience. This reflected the spontaneity of how the Holy Spirit works. Jesus told Nicodemus that the Holy Spirit was like the wind; we can't know where He's come from or where He's going. This unpredictability and freshness contributed greatly to the steady growth of the early church as word got out about their gatherings; people came to see for themselves because they were curious and hungry.

These verses (above) come near the end of a long teaching by Paul to the church in Corinth on how to operate in spiritual gifts when they gather. He tells them to exercise these gifts in an orderly way, so that everyone is encouraged. But the main point is to *exercise them*. Miracles, healings and gifts of revelation like prophecy and speaking in other languages were a regular part of the house church gatherings. The impact of these was huge, both for the believers and for the visiting seekers.

The early church knew the power of spiritual gifts being exercised whenever they gathered; healings, prophecies, and revelations have a powerful impact upon newcomers. Ramsay MacMullen, professor of history at Yale University, after years of studying the remarkable growth of the early church, came to the conclusion that it was these demonstrations of the Spirit that, more than anything else, were responsible for the daily increase of the church.[10]

Jesus said that the Kingdom of Heaven is like leaven, that though it begins so small as to be almost imperceptible, it continually grows until eventually it changes the environment around it. There is no better example or fulfillment of His words than what took place in the first three hundred years of the church. In home after home, without any large-scale meetings, even without permission for public gatherings, the Kingdom was growing through new kinds of communities marked by deep and steady devotion to Christ and to one another, a willingness to live contrary to the values of the surrounding culture, and the powerful presence of God's Spirit in their midst.

It is no wonder that *"the Lord added daily to their number those who were being saved." (Acts 2:47 CSB)*

The essence of the Christian life, of following Jesus, is both faith and practice. Jesus made this clear at the end of his Sermon

---

10 R. MacMullen, *Christianizing the Roman Empire* (Yale University Press, 1984)

on the Mount. "Therefore, everyone who hears these words of Mine and puts them into practice is like a man who built his house on the rock" (Mt 7:24). Jesus' words have to be believed, but they must also be *acted upon*. The apostle James developed this truth in his letter to the church.

> *"What good is it, my brothers, if a man claims to have faith but has no deeds? Can such faith save him?...I will show you my faith by what I do."*
>
> *(Jas 2:14,18 CSB)*

A study of the early church is always very fruitful; it provides an understanding of how the believers, initially taught by those who had most closely lived with and followed the teaching of Jesus, put what they had learned into practice. The early church, while far from perfect, provides a foundation and standard upon which we can build in our time.

It is exciting to gain new knowledge about the Bible or church history. However, this knowledge comes with the responsibility of discovering ways to tangibly apply what we learn. Otherwise, we are in danger of living a theoretical Christianity that makes no real difference to the world around us, and in fact, isolates us from our neighbors.

PUTTING IT INTO PRACTICE

THE AGAPE MEAL
- When sharing a meal in your home, include as part of the meal, the Lord's Supper (also known as the

Eucharist, which means thanksgiving). This is the Biblical context for communion, rather than the small wafer and cup being passed out on Sunday morning (although there is certainly nothing wrong with that). For years in our home, we have experienced a greater depth and intimacy as we have shared the cup and the bread around our table with friends.

- As a First Church or small group, be sure to regularly incorporate the Lord's Supper into your gatherings. Remembering and celebrating the Lord's body and blood is at the historical center of the church, a sacrament pointing to the mystery of the cross.

COUNTER-CULTURAL

- Encourage and challenge each other to reach out to new people who are outside of your usual social network.

- Specifically, reach out to an immigrant family, or a refugee family. Without exception, when we have done this, our invitation has been warmly received. The reality is that most families who have come from another nation have never been invited into the home of a Christian family. On the one hand, this seems almost tragic; on the other, it presents a great opportunity to love and impact many more people.

- Likewise, it is very healthy for us to step across the

comfort of our socio-economic barriers and reach out to a person or family who are living in a lower economic strata. Remember, the early church was marked by its economic diversity.

THE POOR

- There are many ways to reach out and care for poor in our cities. In both the Old and New Testaments, again and again, the Lord specifically tells us to care for the poor. Not only are we enjoined to do this as individuals, it is a key component of an authentic Christian community. We are created to give ourselves away. As our First Churches and small groups prioritize caring for the poor, we find the grace and life of Christ pouring into us in a new way. Frankly, our churches need the poor more than the poor need us.

8

What Makes a First Church?
Part One

"All the believers devoted themselves to the apostles' teaching, and to fellowship, and to sharing in meals (including the Lord's Supper), and to prayer."

Acts 2:42

Now that we have looked at the distinctives of the early church, we will examine how these have been adapted by various First Church models in our time. It is apparent that there are some core values and practices which differ between First Churches and many small group models. The most foundational of these differences revolve around how community, mission and participation are viewed and practiced. For those who have embraced the small group model (which is by far the more prevalent model in the Western church), the values and practices presented in this chapter can easily be adapted. The principles are universal. We must remember, the most important issue is the core agenda that Jesus presented to us, the Great Commission. First Churches and small groups are simply the means of carrying that out.

COMMUNITY

Community is the foundation of all God-breathed activity; abundant life is lived in the context of other people. This is because we are the creation and expression of a God who lives in eternal and continuous community—the Trinity. The early church fathers and mothers knew that an understanding of the Trinity is central to our life in Christ because, without this, we cannot know God rightly. The Trinity is not an aspect of God; the Trinity is who God *is* and who He has always been.

There is no getting around this. If we want to move from meetings to family, from program to deep community, we *must* eat together. A lot.

The Triune God lives in the eternal and infinite inclusion of the Father, Son and Holy Spirit. From ancient times, the activity of the Trinity has been called "the Divine Dance", which expresses the joyful, Other-centered, self-giving love of God. It is this *kenotic* (self-emptying) love that is the creative force which is both the foundation and movement of all creation.

The Trinity embraces both the unity of the Godhead and the individuality of the Father who sends, the Son who is sent, and the Holy Spirit who comes when the Son departs (Jn 16:7). All three Persons of the Godhead celebrate, honor and love one another without losing their individuality. They live in perfect unity and connectedness, and yet are distinct so that each One may live for the sake of the other. Each member is unique, yet fully connected. As Hans Urs von Balthasar has written:

> "Thus, here the principle of individuality—the inviolable prerequisite for any full communion—totally excludes any idea of what we in a world of finite beings would call 'private'".[1]

Community is at the heart of the cosmos, and when we pursue and embrace community, we step into the eternal and infinite life for which we were created. In community, we are moving in the rhythm of the Triune God. When we move in step with Him we find abundant life—life as He intended it to be. It is because our community reflects the Trinity's shared life that we experience supernatural favor. It is not primarily our strategies or even the attraction of our corporate life that causes others to join us (although that is certainly one reason); at its heart, living inclusively is like a God-ordained magnet. This is why Jesus called us a city on a hill; instinctively, people recognize that this shared life is what they are made for.

The heart and strength of community is relationship. As we have seen, the desire for authentic relationship, to really belong, is at the core of every person on the planet. For relationship to be real, it requires fellowship, which is what happens

1 H. Urs von Balthasar, *Engagement With God* (San Francisco: Ignatius Press, 1986), 31

when we spend time together. And in all cultures, one of the clearest expressions of community, of real fellowship, is eating together. Nothing breaks down walls, nothing joins hearts like sharing a meal. That is why it is so vital in First Church that we eat together regularly. There is no getting around this. If we want to move from meetings to family, from program to deep community, we *must* eat together. A lot.

The typical small group has about 10-15 members. In contrast, most First Churches have 40-50 people gathered. This is the result of both the attractiveness of their shared life, and the high value placed upon living inclusively. Because of the steady influx of new people, it would be impossible to keep a First Church small without multiplying every couple of weeks. For years, I embraced the standard view regarding optimum small group size, teaching that if a group got too big it lost both intimacy and individual participation. However, one of the great surprises when I encountered First Churches in India was that, actually, the larger group had much greater energy and a sense of anticipation whenever they gathered. This energy created an environment for *more* people to speak out, pray, testify, and minister.

As Balthasar has stated, to hold onto a preference for privacy, for our individualism, is to deny Christ's life in us. This commitment to live a corporate life, deeply joined to others in a reflection of the activity of our God, is perhaps the most radical and visible sign of being a new community. To live in this way was profoundly counter-cultural in the Roman world; it is the same today. In our day, we live within boundaries, having only limited time to share with others. We tend to set our schedules as a reflection of our priorities—self, career, and family time. We see these as exclusive, rather than as intersection points with our small group.

A few years ago, my wife and I went on vacation to our favorite place on earth—a small cabin in the woods located on an island off the coast of British Columbia. Our First Church all knew where we were going (a few had been there before); they were happy for us to have a vacation. After several days, we started getting texts; one by one, they had decided to join us for the weekend. I don't remember my first reaction to this news, but I know that in earlier years I would have considered this an invasion of Christina's and my vacation. They came on various ferries throughout that Friday, with the last couple arriving after midnight. For the next two days we played, laughed, shared some really deep things, ate (and ate), and prayed. In short, we simply lived life together without plan or agenda. Truthfully, I remember this as one of the best weekends of my life. Honestly. First Church re-defines our lives.

The New Testament uses several metaphors to describe the church: the family of God, the new temple built with living stones, and the body of Christ. All of these describe connectedness and corporality. Paul refers to himself as a father who watches over his family, reminding the church in Ephesus, "You are members of God's family" (Eph 2:19). Peter exhorts his readers to "love the family of believers" (1 Pe 2:17). John, in both his Gospel and first letter, often reminds his readers that they are children of God, born into "God's family" (Jn 1:12; 1

Jn 3:9). The family of God is more than a metaphor; it reflects the actual family life of the early church.

Even a quick reading of Acts reveals the family life of the church. They ate together, and went from house to house, daily living life together. Consider for a moment some of the characteristics of a healthy family. First of all, there is no formality. Family members are encouraged to express themselves freely. There is usually open and honest communication. Families often live with a high degree of spontaneity; that is part of the joy of being a family. Family members share in the daily joys and sorrows of each member. One of my fondest memories of the years when our four sons were still at home was the sharing of life around the dinner table, where each one knew that they were completely free to talk about what was happening in their lives. Throughout their teens and beyond, they brought friends to our home to share in our life together, whether through game nights or joining in the lively dinner discussions. At times, some of their friends lived with us. I think that so many of them became part of our lives because they instinctively knew that they were always welcome and that they could belong.

For over thirty years, we have made a point of having young adults live with us as part of our family. There have been a lot over the years; we consider many to be spiritual sons and daughters. All have enriched us. If we really want to live inclusive lives like Jesus did, then we must make this practical. For many of us, this will mean a fairly significant change, even if it is just opening our homes to one disciple.

Ignatius was a disciple of the Apostle John who went on to become the bishop of Antioch and one of the earliest of the church fathers. In a letter to Polycarp, who was the bishop of Smyrna and a fellow disciple of John, Ignatius described church life:

> "Labor together with one another; strive in company together; run together; suffer together; sleep together; and awake together as the stewards and associates and servants of God."[2]

Ignatius intended this letter to be read to the church in Smyrna. He was exhorting them to continue living closely as family. This did not describe meetings or gatherings, but rather, a lifestyle. Ignatius knew that this whole new kind of community—the church—is not built upon training or even the things that we consider marks of spiritual maturity. What we are called to be is a *family*. When there is real family, people can sense it; they instinctively know that they are in a place of welcome, safety and nurture, where they can grow into who God made them to be.

Several years ago, when I was first trying to understand First Churches, I asked a friend of mine, Anuroop, who leads a First Church network of hundreds of thousands of believers, "How often do First Churches meet?" He replied, "Every day." Surprised, I responded, *"Every day?"* To which he replied, "Well, except for the days when they don't meet." Now I was

2 A. Roberts & J. Donaldson, *Ante-Nicene Fathers* (Peabody, Mass: Hendrickson Publishers, 2012), 95

completely confused. Then Anuroop laughed and told me that he was just messing with me in order to make a point. This is one of the most important things for us to understand about the differences between small groups and First Church. In the West, we define a small group by two factors: the time of the meeting and the location. The same is true for Sunday mornings. The church is largely defined by time and place. Most small groups meet at the same home (usually the leader's) and at the same hour every week.

This presents us with a vitally important and foundational paradigm shift. A First Church is not a meeting; it is the *people* in the First Church (or small group). This was perhaps the single most difficult principle for me to grasp. After decades of only thinking in terms of the house and at what time we are meeting, it took me a long time to begin to instinctively think this way— in fact, I am still in process on this. However, we must get this if we are going to reach people effectively with the truth of the Gospel and bring them into authentic community.

To help me make this paradigm shift from meeting to family, I often used my own experience with my wife, children and grandchildren as a grid for understanding the early church. I would ask myself two questions: *When* are we a family? Always. *Where* are we a family? Everywhere. This is authentic and full church life. This is what the early church knew and what has been re-discovered in much of the church in the developing world.

So, what does this shift look like in a practical way? When

a few of the First Church meet for lunch at McDonalds or KFC (which my Indian friends insist stands for Kingdom Fellowship Center), *this* is First Church; it is not an activity outside of First Church. To become part of First Church is to truly become part of a family. Like all families, it is a family 24/7. It is identified and defined by relationships, not a meeting time. This is why Anuroop said they meet every day. How does this become practical? Two ways stand out: first, when they *do* gather, it tends to be at a different home and time. First Church gatherings happen without a lot of planning or notice. Word of mouth (isn't it good that we live in the mobile phone age!) leads to a lot of fluidity. Secondly, the members share life together, multiple times a week—in each other's homes, out ministering together, eating together, playing together. When we begin to experience this, to *live* this, the result is great joy. In fact, when I first encountered the shared life of the First Church, I phoned back to North America and said to his wife, "I have just met the most joyful Christians I have ever known." Many years later, this testimony has not changed.

It is all too easy for us to overlook just how attractive authentic community really is. I am convinced that this is something very supernatural; whenever we are together, the Triune God is with us; after all, isn't this exactly what Jesus promised: "For where two or three gather in my name, there am I with them" (Mt 18:20). When we are freed from the specific time and place paradigm that we have known, we quickly discover the almost endless expressions of true community that are available to us.

A while ago on our way home from a day of outreach, a group

of us stopped at an outdoor coffee shop. It was one of several shops and restaurants joined in a row. As we had our coffee and snacks, someone began to sing. Immediately, everyone joined in. In almost no time, people began to gather to watch. A group of people singing is, of itself, no big deal; however, when the Holy Spirit is present, there is a supernatural attractiveness. As the crowd continued to gather, one of the team began to share a testimony. Soon, two men from the crowd came forward and asked if they, too, could share a testimony of how Jesus had touched them. And still the crowd grew. We offered to pray for anyone who wanted prayer. Over the next several minutes, we saw eleven people healed and twenty give their lives to Jesus. (Each one shared their contact information and were then contacted the following day and invited to become part of a First Church.) When we realize that we *are* a First Church wherever we go, we no longer have to invite someone to come to a meeting on another day.

It is no wonder that Luke's description of the early church in Acts 2 finishes with "And the Lord added to their number daily". The early church didn't grow because of meetings; it grew because this new way of living life together was so attractive. How did they know to do this? They were replicating how they saw Jesus live for over three years. I am convinced that this is how God intended life to be lived—in a community that reflects the eternal community of the Triune Godhead. It was for this that we were created.

I encourage us to look at this passage again, picturing it not as something from the ancient past, but as our lives today:

They broke bread in their homes and ate together with glad and sincere hearts, praising God and enjoying the favor of all the people. And the Lord added to their number daily those who were being saved.

(Act 2:46-7 NIV)

MISSIONAL

A second foundational way that First Churches differ from small groups is *motivation*. Most small groups in their various forms have a common value: more than anything else they exist for the care, encouragement and support of the group members. Without a strong value on being missional, they tend to be somewhat static, with very little numeric growth (with the possible exception of Sunday church members joining). In contrast, First Churches are built upon a consistent (and passionate) commitment to the *Great Commission* which Jesus gave to his disciples at the end of His ministry, before He ascended to the Father. We have already identified this as His, and therefore His disciples', core agenda.

And Jesus came and said to them, "All authority in heaven and on earth has been given to me. Go therefore and make disciples of all nations, baptizing them in the name of the Father and of the Son and of the Holy Spirit, teaching them to observe all that I have commanded you. And behold, I am with you always, to the end of the age."

(Mt 28:18-20 CSB)

Since writing about my first encounter with First Churches, I have participated in more of them than I can count. I have been to First Churches that gathered in poor villages, farms, urban slums, middle class and upper-middle class homes. Recently, we have established First Churches among the Roma people in Bulgaria. No matter where First Churches meet, at their core lies the Great Commission. Near the end of one of my early encounters with a First Church in northern India, a little girl (about 4 or 5) walked by; as she did so Randeep stopped her: "This is my friend Steve. Can you tell him the Great Commission?" With no hesitation, she looked at me and said, "Certainly Uncle." Jesus said, 'All authority in heaven and on earth has been given to me…'" and she continued to declare the entire passage with confidence and clarity. This is absolutely central to First Churches. And this goes far beyond memorizing some verses. Whenever the First Church gathers, there are *always* new people. Usually they are brought by someone who was new themselves only a few days earlier. Without a doubt, nurture and deep fellowship happen, but it is built upon a foundation of a greater purpose. Jesus' call to make disciples runs very deep in First Churches.

When we truly embrace Jesus' Great Commission, every gathering becomes an opportunity to bring and include someone who has not yet encountered Christ. We are inviting them into a community of both welcome and purpose. First Churches present us with a paradox, something very counter-intuitive. In small groups we are hesitant to enter into outreach and purposeful growth for fear of losing the relational closeness that we enjoy. For over forty years, I have heard this concern expressed from small group members. However, to spend any time with a First Church is to be confronted with the obvious depth of relationships that exist. There is a level of commitment not only to the Great Commission, but to one another that increases in the atmosphere of growth. Experiencing new people coming into the community is exciting, not least because bearing fruit brings glory to the Lord (Jn 15:8). There is a perpetual freshness that comes with new people. Each new person comes with their own unique personality and story, continually breathing new life into everyone else.

Like community, when we share a missional life, we are moving in the rhythm of Jesus. He is the One who told the fishermen, "Come follow Me and I will make you fishers of men." In other words, "There is a job to do." Disciples know that they are on a great cosmic assignment, one with eternal implications. This assignment calls us into action; after all, we are following the One who was continually moving forward, inviting and including everyone He met. A missional community is, of necessity, an inclusive one. Jesus never hung back and waited for people to come to Him. He was the one who came to "seek and to save", no matter where He went. Missional communities live with intention. If we are going to reach people with the beautiful Gospel, then we must go to people. No matter where I am in the world, when I invite churches to come out to the streets with me, I am always met with fear and unbelief. Virtually every church tells me, "that won't work here". I never argue; instead, I simply say, "You're probably right, but let's just try it anyway." Without exception, when we come back to the church, it is filled with amazed and happy people who have just discovered that Jesus really *does* work through them if they will just make themselves available.

They also know that in following Jesus, disciples are stepping into a very real war. Although many believers do not want to acknowledge the existence of spiritual warfare, their reluctance does not negate its reality. As followers of Jesus, we are engaged in a conflict against an enemy who does all that he can to neutralize us, often through indifference and apathy. But when we step into the front lines of Kingdom activity—healing the sick, leading people to Christ, casting out demonic spirits—we quickly discover that it is in the midst of this warfare activity where we find the Holy Spirit connecting us more deeply to our fellow disciples. Ask any soldier and he or she will tell you that the closest, most profound bonds of friendship that they ever experienced were on the battlefield.

It is the mission that reminds us of why we are here on earth as disciples of Jesus. And it is the mission that focuses us as we live life together. We need the mission as much as we need family. Remember the two great universal needs: security *and* significance; without both being met, we wrestle with a sense of incompleteness.

THE SACRIFICE OF THE GENTILES

In 2012, I met Dr. Victor Choudhrie, who pioneered the national house church movement in India, of which Randeep and Anuroop are a part. After traveling for 72 hours in order to meet the man I had heard of ten years earlier, we spent two days together. I asked question after question and Dr. Choudhrie graciously answered them all. Of everything I learned, nothing impacted me more than what he had to say about evangelism. One of the principal ways he taught others to put the Great Commission into practice was through something he called "the sacrifice of the Gentiles". It is a lengthy teaching, but here are the main points:

- The first mention of worship is in Genesis 22 when Abraham took Isaac up Mount Moriah. God told Abraham to offer Isaac as a sacrifice.

- The Old Testament temple was a place of sacrifice. Jews did not enter the temple empty handed. They offered sacrifices at least three times a year. (Note that Mary and Joseph offered two turtle doves at the temple as a sacrifice to dedicate Jesus.)

- In the New Testament, true worship is now to offer ourselves as a living sacrifice (Ro 12:1-2).

- Jesus is our High Priest who has "entered the most holy place once for all, not by the blood of goats and calves, but by His own blood" (Heb 9:12).

- In worship, God still seeks a sacrifice, but in the new covenant, the sacrifice is no longer four-legged, but two-legged.

- When Jesus encountered the Samaritan woman at the well (Jn 4), He told her that from now on, there will be true worship (v. 23). She responded by bringing her whole village to Jesus. This was a defining moment because worship changed: from temple to everywhere; from sacrificing animals to offering Gentiles; and from a professional priesthood to the priesthood of all believers.

- Paul declared to the church, *"...because of the grace given me by God to be a minister of Christ Jesus to the Gentiles, serving as a priest of God's good news. My purpose is that the offering of the Gentiles may be acceptable, sanctified by the Holy Spirit."* *(Ro 15:15,16 CSB)*. The principle has not changed in the new covenant: when we worship, we bring a sacrifice.

When this is taught and modeled, First Churches and small groups of all kinds become temples. Disciples view their gatherings in a whole new way. Each gathering is the "new temple" with Christ in the midst (Mt 18:20). Every First Church network overseer I have spoken with has told me that instilling "the sacrifice of the Gentiles" (i.e. worship) is perhaps the biggest single key to keeping the First Churches focused outward, continually growing with new believers.

In First Church, when someone turns to Christ, he or she is immediately taught the Great Commission and is encouraged to go out and make disciples. On a number of occasions, I have been in First Churches where someone had come as a newcomer only a few days ago and was now bringing one or two others. This should not surprise us; in fact it should be normative. Consider Matthew the tax collector. When he encountered Christ, what was his instinctive response? He invited all his friends to come over to his house to meet Jesus. Instead of expecting new disciples to "sit and learn" until they are more mature, we need to follow the pattern of the early church in the book of Acts. Multiplication did not happen through big evangelistic meetings or programs (which were not allowed), but through releasing joyful new believers to bring and include everyone they encountered. Because this releasing and empowering model is the only one that the new disciples know, they instinctively and eagerly reach out. Evangelism is not something that they are told and taught to do; it is their response to meeting Jesus and to being in a community marked by freedom and celebration.

One of the great strengths of First Church is mutual encouragement among the disciples. Besides teaching each one about the responsibility to present the sacrifice of the Gentiles, there is a power in going out as a group into the mission field of the local neighborhood, park or restaurant, with the specific purpose of releasing the Kingdom of God. Nothing helps a new disciple to step out and pray for a stranger like going with another brother or sister to watch and learn, then to step out themselves. For years I have seen even stagnant groups come alive by simply going out into the community together to pray for the sick, feed the poor or visit the elderly.

While most of the principles upon which First Churches are built can be easily applied to various types of small groups, there is a major difference in how each of these is started. Typically, small groups begin with gathering a number of believers, often from the same church. One of the most surprising aspects of First Churches that I encountered in India is that disciples are sent out from an existing First Church "two by two". No more and no less. In chapter ten, we will look in more detail at how this works. The key point is that, in this model, the only way that a new First Church is established is if the two disciples are successful in gathering unbelievers. If we are in a group consisting of other Christians, we can delay reaching out and we still have a viable group. When there are just two of us, we are highly motivated to be continually going out to reach unbelievers. More than any other principle that I share with churches, this is the most intimidating. Because we spend so much of our time surrounded by other believers, it is hard for us to imagine "not yet" believers coming together. We will look at how to make this shift in more depth later, but for now, begin to consider prayer walking the neighborhood (after finding out *which* neighborhood Jesus is sending you to—see chapter three). Secondly, build intentional hospitality into your schedule; be consistent with this and watch how the Lord opens up new relationships. Those men and women who have established entire networks of First Churches tell me that this is one of the most important principles of all.

PUTTING IT INTO PRACTICE

Transitioning a First Church or small group from a meeting to a family orientation will not happen without a willingness to leave the familiar and comfortable. Likewise with becoming missional. It will take effort and a sense of vision. However, there is great joy and fruitfulness waiting for those who are willing to make the journey.

COMMUNITY

"This commitment to live a corporate life, deeply joined to others in a reflection of the activity of our God, is perhaps the most radical and visible sign of being a new community. To live in this way was profoundly counter-cultural in the Roman world; it is the same today."

1. As a group, frequently engage in discussions about the ways in which you are corporately progressing as a community.

   • In what ways are we functioning like a family? In what ways are we not?

   • How can we change and grow? In what ways are we *willing* to embrace change?

   • Discuss the kinds of activities that make a family what it is. Which of these can we embrace and learn from as a First Church or small group?

2. As individuals, how can we live with a greater sense of community?

MISSIONAL

A First Church that consistently embraces a strong sense of mission is a vibrant, exciting and joyous First Church. Here are a few ways to keep focused:

1. Consistently remind, teach and speak to each other about the Great Commission (see chapter 4).

   - If the Great Commission is going to become a core value of First Church or small group, it must be a seed that is intentionally planted and continually watered in every person.

   - Encourage each other to memorize the Great Commission and recite it together on a regular basis.

2. Often, go over the scriptures related to "the sacrifice of the Gentiles".

3. When there are newcomers, be very welcoming and attentive to them.

   - Listen to their story.

   - *Always* pray for them; give them prophetic words.

   - The newcomer is the VIP in group.

4. Share missional testimonies from that week and celebrate what the Lord did.

5. Commit to going out into the community as a group and as individuals on a regular basis (see chapter five).

6. Instead of meeting at the same home each week, move the group around. This will make it much more likely that neighbors will bc invited to come over and meet the host's friends.

9

What Makes a First Church?
Part Two

*"Let the message about Christ, in all its
richness, fill your lives. Teach and counsel each
other with all the wisdom he gives. Sing psalms
and hymns and spiritual songs to God with
thankful hearts."*

Colossians 3:16

PARTICIPATION

Earlier, I wrote that every person on the planet has been created
with two fundamental needs: security—to be nurtured and to
belong; and significance—the desire to make a difference, to
have an impact. Both of these universal needs are met in a First
Church. We have considered how the First Church as *family*
meets our need for security. Our need for significance is met in
a gathering where everyone is encouraged to participate; in this
environment, we begin to explore who we really are and how

we can impact those around us.

In Paul's first letter to the Corinthians, he gave a lot of attention to what should take place in their gatherings. It is important to remember that he was addressing believers who met regularly in homes. The large, Sunday morning church service was unknown to them all; it would not come into being for another 300 years. Paul summarized his various instructions with this single verse:

> *"When you come together, everyone has a hymn, or a word of instruction, a revelation, a tongue or an interpretation. All of these must be done for the strengthening of the church."*
>
> *(1 Cor 14:26 NIV)*

Consistently in his letters, Paul focuses on the importance of being mutually encouraged and built up whenever the church gathers. Earlier in chapter 14, Paul told them the purpose of New Testament prophecy: edification, encouragement and comfort. Paul knew that the journey of following Jesus is joyful and yet challenging. We need the mutual support and strengthening that results from coming together. In his letter to the Ephesians, Paul reminds the church that it is the connections, like the joints in a body, that "promote the growth of the body for building up itself in love by the proper working of each individual part" (Eph 4:16). Like the Trinity, the church reflects both the unity and the distinctness of each person.

The motive for ministry in First Church is encouragement and edification, but the means for this is the participation of every member—"*everyone* has a hymn, or a word of instruction." Whenever I am with a First Church gathering, I am greatly affected by the sheer energy and faith expressed as, one after another, each participant contributes whatever the Lord has given him or her. It is always beautiful to witness the Lord speaking through everyone. It is like watching a tapestry being woven—by the Holy Spirit, not by a group leader or any other human agent.

In his classic commentary of First Corinthians, Gordon Fee writes:

> "What is striking in this entire discussion is the absence of any mention of leadership or of anyone who would be responsible for seeing that these guidelines were generally adhered to. The community appears to be left to itself and the Holy Spirit."[1]

This model for the corporate gathering is a radical departure from the experience of most believers in the 21st century Western church. Our small group "order of service", which is really just a copy of the only example we have known—the Sunday morning service—can virtually eliminate spontaneity as we seek to make sure that everything is done "decently and in order". If there is one thing that I have learned from forty years of ministry, it is that when He is given room to move, the

---

1 Gordon Fee, *The New International Commentary on the New Testament: First Corinthians* (Grand Rapids MI: Wm B. Eerdmans Publishing, 1987), 691

Holy Spirit more often than not will surprise us. Years ago, a friend of mine who was pastoring a large and rapidly growing church in Ohio told me, "I have discovered that to the extent that I try to make sure that everything is being done right and with excellence, to that degree we stop growing and we start to lose energy. On the other hand, to the degree that I let things go, in spite of my fear, to that degree the Lord moves in our midst and we experience acceleration."

> We have relied on persuasion and human attractiveness to reach unbelievers, when their real need is to witness and experience the reality of His Presence.

In this atmosphere of trust, members step out with confidence that they are hearing the Lord, instead of fearing that they may be corrected for being out of order. As I wrote earlier, I am confident that I will never forget my first First Church meeting where, from beginning to end, person after person stepped out with a song, a scripture, a testimony, a teaching, a prophecy or a prayer. John Wimber used to refer to these various manifestations as "the dancing hand of God." *This* is the ethos of First Church. Without exception, their gatherings are marked by encouragement and freedom. (Remember Paul's exhortation: *"Where the Spirit of the Lord is, there is freedom" (2 Cor 3:17).* This freedom, this joy is infectious. No wonder so many unbelievers when visiting for the first time, know that the Lord is in the midst, and so quickly open their hearts to Jesus.

The church in the West is living in an age where, to various degrees, we are afraid of offending outsiders. This has led to a lot of very safe, tame gatherings where we are in control. And what has the result been? Church attendance in North America has continued to decline every year since 1977. We have forgotten what Paul understood so well: we are all created to experience the love and presence of God. That is why he continually was reminding the various churches that, more than anything, they are the people of the Spirit. We have relied on persuasion and human attractiveness to reach unbelievers, when their real need is to witness and experience the reality of His Presence—His dancing hand

During my first tour of First Churches in India, after witnessing several of these participatory, interactive gatherings, I asked my friend Anuroop how the believers were taught to step out like I was witnessing. His response surprised me: he told me that after about three years of trying to get the believers to move from a passive model where they sat and listened to what the leader taught, they gave up trying to change them. It was simply too difficult to change the patterns of group behavior. Instead, they blessed these believers and encouraged them to continue on in this, their preferred way. Then they started over again. Anuroop and his disciples did not start with Christians; they reached out to unbelievers. As each person would turn to Christ, they would immediately reach out to their friends and family. Before very long, Anuroop had groups of new believers who did not have to "unlearn" anything. From the beginning, even before coming to faith, they learned to recognize the voice of Jesus and then share what each one was hearing. They learned to tell testimonies of what the Lord had done in their lives. They began to speak out the desires of their heart and then discovered that what they were doing was called "prayer". Paul's exhortation that, *"when you come together, everyone has..."* was the only kind of church that they knew. This is what we were made for, what brought deep satisfaction. As Paul wrote to the Ephesians, this work of the Holy Spirit in our midst is simply the down payment of our ultimate inheritance (Eph 1:14). It is this freedom, this embracing of the activity of the Spirit, that makes First Church gatherings so wonderful.

One of the great tenets of the Protestant faith is *the priesthood of all believers*. This was first expressed forcefully by Martin Luther in 1520 in his *Address to the Nobility of the German Nation*[2], and it has remained central to this day. Luther and the Reformers that followed all insisted that there should be no clergy-laity divide. We all have direct access to Christ.

> *But you are a chosen people, royal priests, a holy nation,*
> *a people for God's own possession. You were chosen to*
> *tell about the wonderful acts of God, who called you out*
> *of darkness into his wonderful light.*
>
> *(1 Pe 2:9 NCV)*

Though the priesthood of all believers is theologically adhered to, there is often very limited outworking, even in our small groups. In the participatory model of the First Church, every member functions as a priest, free to "tell about the wonderful acts of God." One of the most striking ways in which this

---

2 http://www.sjsu.edu/people/andrew.fleck/courses/Hum1bSpr15/Lec-ture_25%20Luther_Lotzer_Calvin.pdf

priesthood is lived out is through baptism. Traditionally, when someone turns to Christ, he is invited to attend a new believers or baptism class. These typically last for several weeks (sometimes months). At the completion of the course, the pastor then baptizes the new believer. However, in First Church, as soon as someone turns to Christ, he or she is immediately baptized. (See chapter 2.) Just as significantly, the baptism is performed not by the pastor, but the person who led the new believer to the Lord. Often this means that a person who has been a disciple for only a few days is now the one doing the baptizing. One of the many strengths of First Church is that it facilitates everyone putting the Gospel into practice from the first day. This leads to confident, active disciples who are experiencing the fulfillment of their destiny, and not just sitting and hearing teaching about how one day they will be ready to step out.

During the past six years, I have taken over 200 people to northern India on Journeys of Compassion. Every one of them heals the sick, leads men, women and children to a relationship with Jesus, and provides food, clean water and medical care to thousands. Yet, at the end of every trip when I ask for their favorite memory, most often they say: "It was watching and participating in First Churches that was the best of all!"

Paul vividly captures some of what it is like to be joined with others in the community, mission and participation of First Church:

> *"Let the Word of Christ—the Message—have the run of the house. Give it plenty of room in your lives. Instruct*

and direct one another using good common sense. And
sing, sing your hearts out to God! Let every detail in
your lives—words, actions, whatever—be done in the
name of the Master, Jesus, thanking God the Father
every step of the way."

(Col 3:16-17, MSG)

This is the way of doing church that has continued to multiply for the past 25 years, so that now there are almost a million disciples in northern India who, throughout the week, participate with brothers and sisters in this joyful, spontaneous, and powerful journey with Christ.

THE RELATIONAL BIBLE STUDY

Whenever I teach pastors and leaders in various nations, I always tell them this: Gospel is always *inclusive*; religion is always *exclusive*. Very few of us recognize those areas in the practicing of our faith where we are actually being exclusive. It is deeply ingrained in us to have a dualistic worldview where we see others as them or us; right or wrong; in or out. It is all too easy for our small groups to be sub-cultural instead of counter-cultural. As a result, when new people come into our gatherings, they instinctively feel like outsiders. If our small groups are not growing, that is one of the reasons.

There is a practice that, although most of us do not realize it, is profoundly exclusive—the Bible study. It isn't that Bible study is itself exclusive (in fact, it is a vital part of our mutual growth and encouragement). Rather, it is the *way* we approach Bible study that is the problem. Typically, the group either works through a book of the Bible, chapter by chapter each week, or it discusses the message that was preached on the previous Sunday, usually with questions provided by the pastor.

Here is the problem: imagine you have been invited by a friend to come to the gathering. You are not yet a Christian, but you are curious to see what your friend is a part of. There may be some singing, and sharing of testimonies. So far, so good. But now the leader tells everyone to open to, for example, Ephesians Chapter Three to continue with the study that has been going on for the past several weeks. Suddenly, your comfort level plummets. You have never read the Bible. You don't even know what an "Ephesians Chapter Three" is. What if you get asked a question? Before it even starts, you are feeling stupid. Or what if the leader says, "Now we're going to discuss the Sunday sermon." You weren't there on Sunday. In fact, you haven't been to *any* church since you went to the local church for the Christmas Eve service two years ago. Immediately, you are on the outside looking in. The group knows something you don't know. Though it is often unintentional, religion is always exclusive.

Here is another way: The Relational Bible Study

There are so many advantages to this approach. It is built upon participation. Everyone takes part instead of one teacher and a room full of listeners. The relational Bible study allows for a level playing field. There are no experts because the scripture passage teaches itself. The Holy Spirit teaches through the group members, sometimes *every one of them*, regardless of whether they are new believers or even non-believers. This leads to a high level of engagement by everyone. In this atmosphere, each person learns to better recognize the work and presence of God in their midst. The relational Bible study also reflects the limitless creativity of God. Though I have led passages like the woman caught in adultery (Jn 8) and Jesus encountering Zacchaeus many times, every time there are new insights revealed; no two studies are ever the same. By letting the Holy Spirit teach the group through the Bible passage, the leader no longer needs to spend hours preparing a weekly teaching, hoping to present something that is profound.

A relational Bible study works something like this: Someone reads an episode from the Gospels. Read it all the way through. Pick one that isn't too long but has obvious meaning and impact. Here are a few examples, but there are many more:

- John 8, The woman caught in adultery.
- Luke 19, Zacchaeus
- Luke 7, The immoral woman in the home of Simon
- Mark 5, Jairus and his daughter
- The parables

Before going on, set out a few ground rules:

1. Only discuss what the passage actually says; don't refer to other places in the Bible to reinforce what you are saying. Remember, we want this to be inclusive and non-threatening for everyone. It really is okay for the

newcomer to have never read the Bible; this guideline keeps everyone on a level playing field.

2. There are no wrong answers. This is very important because otherwise, people will feel nervous about participating.

3. Encourage everyone's input. It is always okay to "pass", but as a leader, make sure that you are asking everyone for their thoughts at several points during the study.

After reading the passage, ask everyone to state in one sentence how the passage made them feel. Then go back and read it verse by verse. Then ask for a response to each verse. Do not be overly directive in your questions; the goal is simply to free people up to share their thoughts. Over the years, no matter how many times I have led the same relational Bible study, every time there are new insights. Often the best ones come from newcomers who have never read the Bible. I remember during a relational Bible study I was leading in Canada that an elderly Hindu man said, "I don't think that anyone can truly forgive unless they have experienced forgiveness." This is the work of the Holy Spirit.

What I love about the relational Bible study is that there is always a point when the group becomes really engaged. Often after just a few minutes, they are all trying to get a word in; in their enthusiasm, they often get louder. There is a great freedom that is unlocked that impacts almost every person in the group. When this happens, the leader should say almost nothing.

Given these guidelines, here is a brief illustration of how an actual relational Bible study might go (at least this time!).

> Leader: Tonight, let's talk about a time when Jesus encountered a woman who had just been caught in adultery (Jn 8:2-11).

(Read the passage in its entirety.)

> Leader: What were you feeling as we read this?

(vv. 2-3)

> What do you think the crowd was feeling? What about the Pharisees?

> If *you* were this woman, what would *you* be feeling?

(It is interesting to see how the men and women in the group often express quite different feelings at this point.)

Give time for people to interact with each other as some will describe the woman's primary feeling as fear; others will say shame; some may say anger. Do the minimum of talking; the Holy Spirit is using the group members (including newcomers) to speak.

(vv. 4-6)

> How did the Pharisees feel about the woman? What was

most important to them at this point?

(vv. 6-7)

Why did Jesus decide to stoop down? What do you think He was writing?

Why did Jesus choose these words? What was His intent?

(vv. 8-9)

Why did all of the people slip away? Why was it the older ones who went first?

What was the crowd feeling now?

(vv. 10-11)

'What was Jesus' tone of voice, His attitude, as He spoke to the woman?

Look closely at v. 11. What do you think Jesus meant by, "Neither do I condemn you. Go, and sin no more."? If there isn't a significant response, you may want to ask, "Was this a correction or a promise?"

Ask the group how they felt about the Bible study. What stands out us? What new insights have we learned? Be sure to reinforce that the Holy Spirit has used each one of us to teach;

that He was leading our discussion. The relational Bible study often leads to talking about the forgiveness of Jesus, how He offers us the healing that comes with forgiveness. This leads beautifully into people pairing up and praying for one another.

Approaching Bible study this way contributes to the overall goal of 1 Cor 14:26. When we gather, *everyone* has a part to play, a contribution that is uniquely theirs. This also keeps us from a theoretical approach to Bible study where we simply learn information. Instead, each one is engaged, and as the highly interactive discussion leads to ministry and prayer, our lives are greatly impacted and enriched. Repeatedly, people have told me that this way of studying the Bible made it come alive in a new and vibrant way, and that they have never understood the passage as well as now.

PUTTING IT INTO PRACTICE

In First Church, where the members are new disciples (and not-yet disciples), it is fairly easy to have a highly participatory gathering because this is the only model anyone has ever known. For those in a small group, where the members have been together for a long time and are all part of a more traditional church model, developing participation is more of a challenge. Though the process may be slower for the small group, it is possible to increase participation.

1. Whoever is the leader must learn how to pull back, to be less directive.

- Do less teaching and more facilitating.

- In the beginning, make it your role to draw others out with their testimonies, prayers, scriptures that spoke to them that week etc.

2. Encourage people to hear God in the gathering.

   - Never leave the gathering without having everyone ask the Lord for a specific word for another person, then have each one pray for the other.

   - Have each one ask Jesus to show them something good or special about the other person, then speak that to them.

3. For a newcomer, pick a simple and short passage from the Gospels and invite him or her to read it out loud. You may then want to ask them to share what the passage means to them. Thus, from the beginning, the new disciple is understanding that her contribution is valued.

4. Consciously develop an ethos of encouragement and freedom in First Church. There are no mistakes.

10

Luke 10: The Central Strategy

"Pray to the Lord of the harvest to send out
laborers into His harvest."

Luke 10:2

The First Church gathering had just finished. I was with over 30 others, mainly from a poor neighborhood in a large city. As people lingered, some visiting, a few praying for others, Randeep called a young girl (about 8 or 9 years old) over and asked her to explain to me how to make disciples. I will always remember her response: "Certainly, Uncle. Jesus gave us the best model for making disciples in Luke 10. First, he told us to go where He is about to go. That means that before we go out, we must ask Him where He is about to go. But don't worry Uncle, He is always going somewhere!" She then proceeded to take me step by step through the principles laid out in Luke 10:1-9. This little girl did this without prior warning or preparation: she simply expressed what had been established in her heart and mind.

This was my first encounter with practical teaching on Luke 10. Over the past six years, whenever I have traveled to Indian First Church, I have come to realize that this is the foundational teaching for the First Church movement. It is something that is taught repeatedly; the leaders recognize the power and necessity of repetition—this is something we can learn from our Indian brothers and sisters. In fact, rarely am I in a gathering, either a First Church or leaders' training, where Luke 10 is not emphasized. I now teach these principles to pastors, church members and church planters in many nations. Yet, as I share these concepts with others, I am discovering that there is always more for me to learn about this model. Discipleship is a very deep well.

After this the Lord appointed seventy-two others and sent them two by two ahead of him to every town and place where he was about to go. He told them, "The harvest is plentiful, but the workers are few. Ask the Lord of the harvest, therefore, to send out workers into his harvest field. Go! I am sending you out like lambs among wolves. Do not take a purse or bag or sandals; and do not greet anyone on the road.

"When you enter a house, first say, 'Peace to this house.' If someone who promotes peace is there, your peace will rest on them; if not, it will return to you. Stay there, eating and drinking whatever they give you, for the worker deserves his wages. Do not move around from house to house.

Luke 10: The Central Strategy

"When you enter a town and are welcomed, eat what is offered to you. Heal the sick who are there and tell them, 'The kingdom of God has come near to you'."

(Lu 10:1-9 NIV)

The "Luke 10 strategy" is applicable beyond planting new First Churches; it is highly instructive for any small group, family, or individual who wants to obey the Great Commission that Jesus gave to us all. Whether you live in a city in the Western world, in a village in the developing world, among the rich or poor, young or old—there are powerful tools found in this passage.

Just like the young girl instructed me, we begin by praying and asking Jesus where He wants us to go. As always, we are learning to follow Jesus; we are not asking Him to follow us. This takes us back to the issue of learning to listen, confident in Jesus' promise that His sheep hear His voice (Jn 10:27). For many years, this has been a principle that I have been committed to growing in. On a large scale, there are more nations and certainly more communities than our organization, Impact Nations, can ever possibly go to. Therefore, we diligently pray over every invitation. And when we are in a nation and are ministering in communities, we continue to pray and ask Jesus if He wants us to be established there, or to move on to where He is moving (Lu 10:10-11). Locally, in my own city, I am often asking Him where He wants me to go to prayer walk and minister in homes. We must remember that God has not placed us randomly, but strategically; therefore, it seems that He usually has prepared people for us where we live or our group gathers.

Jesus sent them out in pairs. This often-overlooked principle is actually very important. There is a strength in agreement that happens when two people are praying. Jesus promises whenever two are gathered, He will be in their midst. Multiple Old Testament passages (e.g. Dt 32:30; Eccl 4:12) state the strength that comes in being joined to another. There are a number of other practical reasons for going out in pairs. If one person becomes discouraged (a favorite tactic of our enemy), the other can build him up, preventing either of them from turning back. While one person is talking to an individual or family, the second one is praying. Also, two people sharing is often more impactful than a single person.

BIND THE STRONGMAN

What do we do when we go out? First and foremost, we are praying. Before anything else, we are shifting the spiritual atmosphere. As we walk, we are asking the Holy Spirit to show us the spiritual strongholds over the area. Jesus told us that we must bind the strongman before we can plunder his goods (winning people to Christ).

> *Who is powerful enough to enter the house of a strong man like Satan and plunder his goods? Only someone even stronger—someone who could tie him up and then plunder his house.*
>
> *(Mk 3:27 NLT)*

When we are prayer walking, we are engaged in spiritual warfare by pushing back the enemy's territory and advancing the Kingdom of God. This starts with discerning the strongholds and then using our authority in Christ to bind them. As we walk by a house or even a whole block, we may suddenly be aware of alcoholism, despair, domestic violence, sickness, or some other stronghold. Like Daniel in chapter nine (Dn 9:4-20), we may find ourselves identifying in our spirits with what has held these families in bondage and then repenting on their behalf (and our own). After addressing and binding these, we then pray in the opposite spirit, releasing specific blessing from heaven. We pray for peace, for reconciliation in families, for financial freedom, and for health. This is our assignment because it is only the Lord's sons and daughters who can release the Father's blessing.

In Psalm 2:8, the Father says to the Son:

> *"Ask of Me, and I will make the nations Your inheritance*
> *and the ends of the earth your possession." (CSB)*

Now, Jesus is sending us out in the same way ("As the Father sent Me, so am I sending you." Jn 20:21). From the time of Abraham, God has told us how important it is to possess the land. It isn't the real estate that matters; it is the men, women and children that the land represents. In prayer walking, we are declaring ownership of every home and business for the Lord. There is great authority in this kind of prayer.

The second thing we pray for is harvest workers. In this passage from Luke, Jesus didn't actually say "pray". Twice in the Gospels He uses the much stronger word: *deomai.* It means to beseech, implore, or even to beg. This is not a casual prayer; it is filled with urgency. With all of our being, we are to cry out to the Lord. And for what? Harvest workers. It is interesting that Jesus never tells us to pray for revival, or even the harvest—prayers that we can distance ourselves from, leaving it up to the Lord or others to fulfill. But when we implore Him for harvest workers, we are acknowledging our personal responsibility to identify and raise up harvest workers. As we prayer walk, we are asking to see people as Jesus sees them, as potential harvest workers.

> "When you guys started coming here a year and a half ago, most of us were afraid to step out our front doors. Now we visit and talk together all the time. And all the gangs and drug dealers have left."

Making disciples and establishing First Churches *is* plundering. In the West, we have a much less definite understanding of the reality of spiritual warfare; as a result, we can easily become enthused and go out to "win the lost" without dealing with our adversary. We forget what Paul warned us:

> *For our struggle is not against flesh and blood, but against the rulers, against the authorities, against the powers of this dark world and against the spiritual forces of evil in the heavenly realms.*
>
> *(Eph 6:12 CSB)*

On many occasions I have seen this "binding the strong man" in action. We see people healed by Jesus, then we invite them to open their hearts to Him. Sometimes, to our surprise, they tell us they are not interested. So, this is what we do: If we are in a foreign nation, we will tell the translator not to interpret while we (all the while smiling benignly) rebuke the enemy and bind his work in this person. Then, we will ask the person (who is unaware of what has just happened) once again if he or she would like to open their lives to Christ. I cannot think of a single time when that same person has not now said "yes" to Jesus. Once again, Paul's words remind us of the true nature of the battle we are in—

"The god of this age has blinded the minds of unbelievers, so that they cannot see the light of the gospel that displays the glory of Christ, who is the image of God."

(2 Cor 4:4 NIV)

This applies to neighborhoods and cities as well as individuals. We have seen housing projects, villages and even a community of over ten thousand radically transformed. A number of years ago, we specifically went to the neighborhood with the highest crime rate and violence in our city. It was dominated by dangerous gangs and drug dealers. We began by praying, then simply demonstrating the love of Jesus, coming in the opposite spirit. We kept praying and loving by serving them. About eighteen months later, while a group of us were there, someone walked up to one of our team and said, "When you guys started coming here a year and a half ago, most of us were afraid to step out our front doors. Now we visit and talk together all the time. And all the gangs and drug dealers have left." Prayer walking is powerful. If we are going to effectively establish

First Churches, lead people to freedom in Christ, and make disciples, we *must* begin with concerted prayer that changes the atmosphere.

Our enemy is very real, and he dominates primarily through controlling thoughts and emotions. Anger, suspicion, fear and indifference are not people's personality flaws—they are strongholds in their lives. Prayer walking helps us begin to perceive people and situations with spiritual eyes, rather than limit our observations to the natural realm.

The first instruction that Jesus gives after sending the 72 out, is to "pray to the Lord of the harvest for workers." For years I assumed that we were to pray for more workers in the church. (This has been a favorite recruiting verse in most churches.) However, I have come to see that what we are really asking the Lord for is *new* harvest workers. We are asking for new believers who will immediately become disciples who in turn make other disciples—harvest workers!

THE HOUSE OF PEACE

The other primary motivation for prayer walking is to identify the house of peace (Lu 10:6). This is the key to planting First Churches. In fact, if the goal is to advance the Kingdom through making disciples in our communities (and it is), then finding the person or house of peace is imperative. There are numerous examples of the person of peace in the New Testament; among them was Lydia who invited Paul into her home in Philippi, and Cornelius who invited Peter into his home. It is important to note that the Gospel spread throughout the Roman world not only through the work of the apostles and evangelists, but equally through houses of peace where churches were established in their homes—which were the only places where the early church met.

The house of peace is the place that the Lord has prepared before we ever arrive. It is the place where there is a person of influence and trust in the community. The person of peace is the one to whom other people are naturally attracted; they are often people of influence. God has already prepared a whole network of relationships through them. This is why Jesus said: *"Don't move around from home to home. Stay in one place, eating and drinking what they provide. Don't hesitate to accept hospitality" (vv. 7,8).* When we find the house of peace, this becomes our focus and our base for ministry. It is often surprising just how quickly others come to us when we are in a house of peace. I remember one afternoon in Canada when I responded to an invitation from a family of peace. They were not Christians, but when I went to visit them, they immediately opened up about their lives and began asking me questions. As I shared some of my story with them, every few minutes different ones would leave the room. I only realized later that they were phoning friends and other family members. I recall that eventually, 22 people were crowded into their front room, where I was able to testify and pray for them. A few months ago, while I was in Bulgaria, some friends and I were invited to the home of a Roma (gypsy) family. Again, before long, there was a whole group of their friends and family gathered to hear about Jesus. We shared our testimonies, told a story from the

Gospels and prayed for the sick. A woman with a tumor the size of an orange went back to the doctor to prepare for surgery and was informed that she no longer had a tumor. She told others what Jesus had done and they wanted to know more. Now there is a First Church.

For years I would prayer walk, asking the Lord to show me the house of peace in the neighborhood. Quite literally, I would pray and walk for many months, waiting for the person of peace to be revealed. I don't know what I was expecting to see—maybe a blue orb hanging over a specific house. At any rate, nothing ever seemed to happen. So, I asked my Indian friends how they identified the house of peace that the Lord had prepared. There answer was simple and practical: the person of peace is the one who invites you into their home. It is that simple! We prayer walk until someone reaches out to us, just like Lydia welcomed Paul and Silas. This took the mystery out of prayer walking.

When we find the house of peace, we have found a powerful tool in the Lord's hand. Again and again, I have visited houses of peace and heard their testimonies of how God has used them for purposes beyond what they could ever have imagined. Randeep shared the following story with me:

> One of my disciples and I were on a prayer walk in a slum in Kinnaur. We had prayer walked that area for two hours. It was very cold and was getting dark. A small woman, a Nepali roadside worker, came and said "What are you doing over here?" We said, "we are praying." She responded: "Why don't you come inside and pray?

It's cold." As we entered her house, we were praying. She went into her kitchen and boiled some eggs, then peeled the shells off the eggs and brought them to the eight of us, carrying them in her hands. It was dark, but when we shined our flashlights to pick up the eggs, we saw that they were all black because she had not washed her hands. We thought: "What should we do?" My disciple said, "Well, brother, the word of God says, eat everything that is set before you." So we ate it. Nothing happened to us; we were fine. As a result, her life changed. She came to Christ and led many others to the Lord. How do you spell fellowship? "FOOD". There is no fellowship without food.

This lady worked as a roadside worker, so she interacted with a lot of people. She won her whole colony to the Lord and started bringing them to the house church. We started sending them to different house churches. Then she was given the job as caretaker of an apple orchard. There, she became very friendly with the seven-year-old son of the owner. One morning she woke up to hear people crying and mourning. The night before, a snake had bitten the boy and he had died. So, in the morning they found the boy dead. When she heard about this, she went and picked up the boy and started running, saying over and over for about 15 minutes, "Jesus, give this boy back to me." People were running after her as she was running with the boy in her arms. After 15 minutes, the boy came back to life; that started another move up, down, and all over that village

Now this Nepali woman is a wonderful church planter. She was illiterate, but she went into a literacy program and now she can read the Bible. This Nepali woman has now baptized over 15,000 people.

This testimony illustrates several points: first, everything begins with prayer walking. We need the Holy Spirit to go before us and open up the house of peace. Secondly, in every culture, it is important to receive people's hospitality; this includes eating whatever they offer (Lu 10:8). It was the power of unconditional acceptance (even though her eggs were black with dirt) which opened up this lady's heart to the love of Jesus. Remember, the cornerstone of the Gospel is to *demonstrate* the love of God, not just talk about it. Thirdly, like all of us, this woman was created with a great destiny. It took Randeep and his friend's willingness to step out in faith that unlocked this destiny. Ephesians 3:20 says,

> *"Now to Him who is able to do above and beyond all that we ask or think according to the power that works in us—to Him be glory in the church." (CSB)*

No one, while prayer walking in this neighborhood, could ever have imagined what Jesus had prepared for this woman. Imagine: 15,000 new disciples and a child risen from the dead—all because two men stepped out in obedience and faith.

Since God has prepared a house of peace, another reason to stay focused there is to avoid becoming distracted. Jesus' words to His disciples carry an urgency:

Luke 10: The Central Strategy

Now go, and remember that I am sending you out as lambs among wolves. Don't take any money with you, nor a traveler's bag, nor an extra pair of sandals. And don't stop to greet anyone on the road. (vv. 3,4 CSB)

Our adversary tries to intimidate us through fear and discouragement. If those tactics don't work, he tries to distract us, either by getting us focused on other things or by spreading ourselves too thinly. I have watched this happen too many times to count. We begin to see God moving in one home and so, too quickly, we launch out to find more fruitful places. Jesus' words remind us, once again, that this is serious warfare in which we are engaged. This passage also reveals a sense of immediacy. We don't need to wait for anything in order to begin. We don't need to have enough money or goods. Just start. Jesus said something similar in John's Gospel: "Don't say four months until the harvest. The fields are ripe now" (Jn 4:35). In other words, we don't need more training or conferences. The Lord has already prepared houses of peace to serve as front-line stations through which we advance the Kingdom of God.

So, how long should we stay at the house of peace? We stay until a First Church has been firmly established in that home. This starts with accepting hospitality. It is interesting how many episodes in the four Gospels center around the meal table. Jesus was very comfortable to accept hospitality, knowing how powerful it is to eat together. Through time spent together around the table, walls come down, and real issues leading to teachable moments present themselves. So, eat together. Often.

161

When determining the right time to leave the First Church in the care of the new leader, look at some of the following indicators:

- Is the group being interactive, asking lots of questions, with everyone participating? Are people sharing freely with testimonies, songs, scriptures etc.?

- Are spiritual gifts, and signs and wonders taking place?

- Is the group regularly active in outreach, both corporately and individually?

- Does the group have a high value on care for the poor, the widow and the orphan?

- Is the group progressing in prayer?

- Are new people coming into the First Church and coming to Christ on a regular basis? Is the group growing numerically?

- Are people growing in maturity?

HEAL THE SICK

Jesus finishes this passage in Luke by telling the 72 that He is sending them out to "Heal the sick who are there and tell them, 'The Kingdom of God has come near.'" Here is the other great key for establishing a First Church: pray for the sick in that home. This may be the person of peace, or it may be a friend or neighbor. Remember, the house of peace is the one already prepared by the Lord; it is the place where neighbors regularly congregate. As soon as one person is healed, the news spreads like wildfire. I have experienced this again and again, in North America and all over the developing world. When we are first at the table visiting, we tell some of our story, or we tell about something that we have seen Jesus do recently. Storytelling is the most effective means of communicating and connecting with others. It naturally leads to asking if anyone needs healing. Because the Holy Spirit has led us to this home and He is in our midst, people soon begin to open up about their needs or sicknesses.

Just a few months ago, I was invited into a home in a poor village in Bulgaria. The family asked me to pray for two sick family members. As the Lord touched them, they became very excited and the mother and aunt opened their hearts and lives to the Lord. But one of the children had slipped out of the house and told a few others what had happened. When my friend and I came out onto the porch, there were almost twenty people waiting for prayer! As we prayed (and the Lord graciously kept healing), people came from all over. I remember looking up and counting 37 people gathered around us; just moments later, I lost count at 50. That was just our first day in that community! Today, there is a First Church, which I expect will be the prototype for many more.

"Tell them the Kingdom of God has come near." What marks

us as the body and family of Christ is not doctrine, but a living relationship with a supernatural God. This is why Paul wrote, "The Kingdom is not in word, but in power" (1 Cor 4:20). I have never been to a First Church gathering where the sick were not prayed for. Likewise, every gathering I have attended has included the practice of various spiritual gifts. It is these that demonstrate to unbelievers that Jesus is real and present. When someone is healed, questions about the reality of God immediately dissolve. I think this is why Jesus instructed the 72, and us to be sure to pray for the sick right from the beginning of our relationship with a new family.

In the West, even among charismatic and Pentecostal churches, I have noticed a steady decrease in the practice of spiritual gifts. We doctrinally agree with the gifts of the Holy Spirit, but our practice of these gifts has become limited. Rarely do I hear of a congregation that is being taught with any depth about spiritual gifts. Yet, in the early church they were central. Church historians have concluded that healing and deliverance are two primary reasons for the explosive growth of the church in the Roman world (see chapter seven). In communities around the world, I have witnessed that this is still true today. We were created for supernatural encounter with God. To downplay or even bypass that truth is to settle for too small a Gospel, and to miss establishing First Churches that will transform communities. Since spiritual gifts were so central in the life of the early church, and continue today in the First Church movement, in the next chapter we will briefly examine spiritual gifts as presented by the apostle Paul.

PUTTING IT INTO PRACTICE

1. Continually be reminding the First Church or small group about the principles that Jesus presents in Luke 10:1-9.

    • Often do a relational Bible study based on this passage. My friend Anuroop once told me that, although he has done this study hundreds of times, every time the Lord brings some new revelation, often through a newcomer who has not yet come to Christ.

    • Encourage members to highlight the various principles presented in Luke 10.

2. Reinforce the purposes and methods of prayer walking among the group.

3. Every couple of months, have the First Church leave the home and go out in pairs. Scatter around the neighborhood and prayer walk.

    • Have each of the pairs report back to the group with what they have discerned.

    • What are the strongholds in the neighborhood, or on a particular street?

- Has the Lord revealed a house of peace? Was contact made during the prayer walk? Did you have an opportunity to pray for the people in the house?

4. Consider the indicators of a healthy First Church presented in this chapter.

    - Discuss how well the group is doing with each of these indicators.

    - Use these indicators as a tool to grow in maturity as a group.

11

Spiritual Gifts in First Church

*"Pursue love and be eager for the spiritual
gifts, especially that you may prophesy."*

1 Corinthians 14:1

His was my oldest friendship, going back to high school. When, as a young married man, I gave my life to Christ, Paul headed for the hills. Now that I was a Christian, he wanted nothing to do with me. After more than a year without contact, Paul called me and said he wanted to talk. This began a series of discussions that went on for a few weeks. Sometimes I had an answer, but usually I had to get back to him. Although he fully acknowledged the change in my life, nothing I said about the reality of Jesus convinced him. One evening, the young adults at my church were having an international potluck dinner. Paul was a bachelor and I was fairly sure he wouldn't turn down a free meal; I was right. After supper, someone pulled out a guitar and we all started to sing worship songs. Paul, who was a musician, seemed to be comfortable. After a while, without human prompting, we began to "sing in the Spirit", which is the term we used in those days for singing in tongues. I was aware that this might be too much for Paul, but there really wasn't anything I could comfortably do about it. Paul stayed until the end. The next day he asked to see me; he said, "I had an explanation for every answer you have given me over the past few weeks. I have no explanation for what took place last night, but somehow I know that God was there."

When Jesus told the Twelve to make disciples, they were to teach others everything that He had taught them. This included healing the sick and setting the spiritually harassed free. There was nothing optional about this. Repeatedly, Jesus had explained to them that they were in a war against the "god of this world". There are two realms: the kingdom of darkness and the Kingdom of God. With every healing, with every deliverance, the Kingdom of God advances.

> *"If I drive out demons by the finger of God, then the Kingdom of God has come upon you."*
> *(Lu 11:20 NKJV))*

Spiritual gifts are not meant to be optional; neither are they simply what Christians do when they gather. Spiritual gifts are manifestations of the Holy Spirit by which God's Kingdom breaks into this realm. The first century church was known for spiritual gifts. Today, wherever I travel in the developing world where the church is experiencing explosive growth, their gatherings are marked by the very active practice of exercising spiritual gifts.

The two fullest descriptions of spiritual gifts and their practice in church gatherings are found in First Corinthians, in chapters 12 and 14.

> *"Now concerning spiritual gifts, brothers and sisters, I do not want you to be uninformed... Now there are varieties of gifts, but the same Spirit; and there are varieties of services, but the same Lord; and there are varieties of activities, but it is the same God who activates all of them in everyone. To each is given the manifestation of the Spirit for the common good. To one is given through the Spirit the utterance of wisdom, and to another the utterance of knowledge according to the same Spirit, to another faith by the same Spirit, to another gifts of healing by the one Spirit, to another the working of miracles, to another prophecy, to another the discernment of spirits, to another various kinds of tongues, to another the interpretation of tongues. All these are activated by one and the same Spirit, who allots to each one individually just as the Spirit chooses."*
>
> *(1 Cor 12:1, 4-11 ESV)*

Paul begins this description by stressing the importance of spiritual gifts. For him, spiritual gifts are not something peripheral to the activity of the church; rather, they are central. Paul then goes on to stress that, although there is a wide variety of gifts, they all come from the Spirit, and he gives them to *everyone* (v. 6). Earlier, I stated that God speaks and moves through even people who do not yet know him. My friend, Anuroop, regularly invites unbelievers to close their eyes and ask Jesus to show or say something. People *always* hear Him speak or reveal a picture in their minds. Again, learning to hear the voice of Jesus is the foundation of all discipleship. For me, I have many times invited unbelievers to join me in praying for the sick. After watching me, I then encourage them to lay hands on the person's pain and then pray in the name of Jesus. They always see Him heal. The Holy Spirit gives gifts to *everyone*, and from our first time in the house of peace, we want the people to both experience and expect God to move.

And why are these gifts given? For the common good. For the building up and encouragement of the church. The Holy Spirit builds up, encourages and directs better than any of our programs or meeting outlines ever could. That is why Paul wrote:

> *"My speech and my proclamation were not with persuasive words of wisdom but with a powerful demonstration by the Spirit, so that your faith might not be based on men's wisdom but on God's power."*
>
> *(1 Cor 2:4-5 CSB)*

In 1 Corinthians 12, Paul lists some of the types of gifts that the church can expect. The nine spiritual gifts that he lists in this passage are not exhaustive. They are representative of a wide variety of spiritual gifts that the Holy Spirit bestows. It is my conviction that spiritual gifts reside *in* the Holy Spirit. Through our faith and willingness to step out, we have access to these gifts, but they don't belong to us; they belong to Him. However, as we remain faithful to exercise them, we grow in anointing, confidence and authority.

Much can be written about each of these spiritual gifts; however here is a brief description of each one:

- **Word of wisdom:** is an utterance inspired by God and spoken by an individual. It is seeing what God sees in a situation and speaking it out. It is applying God's wisdom to a certain situation. Expect a word of wisdom in giving counsel, or in proclaiming the scriptures.

- **Word of knowledge:** is a supernatural revelation of information by the Holy Spirit. It is a fragment of knowledge freely given by God about a person, situation, physical condition etc. that you could not otherwise know through the efforts of your natural mind.

- **Gift of faith:** is the sudden surge of confidence and certainty that God is about to move in a clear way through word or action. It involves both supernatural certainty of God's intervention, and the authority to affect this intervention through the power of the Holy Spirit.

- **Gifts of healing:** is the actual event of healing which a sick person receives. Since there are many kinds of illnesses, there are different healing manifestations. Often healing comes through the laying on of hands or by speaking a word of healing. Healing was central to Jesus' ministry and central to His instructions to His disciples.

- **The working of miracles:** literally, this is "workings of powers (*dunamis*)" and refers to those extraordinary times when God's power breaks in through the actions or words of an individual. It may include raising someone from the dead, changing water into wine, the sudden growing of a limb or eye. The difference between miracles and healings is understood in different ways. For some, miracles are spectacular healings—like when a crippled person suddenly gets up, or a blind person sees. For others, miracles involve God creating something that wasn't there before.

- **Prophecy:** is simply hearing what the Lord says, and then repeating that to others. It does not require any kind of verbal formula. Paul reminds us in 1 Cor 14:3 that, like all other spiritual gifts, its purpose is to build up, encourage, and comfort others. Prophecy is less about foretelling and more about expressing the heart of God for someone in a particular situation. Prophecy in First Church is a sign for believers, revealing that God is present in the midst of their gathering by drawing the attention of the hearer toward God. In 1 Cor 14:22-25, Paul reminds us that prophecy is also a very powerful sign to unbelievers

- **Discerning of spirits:** is a supernatural perception into the spiritual realm for the purpose of determining the source of spiritual activity. It is vital in prayer walking, allowing us to discern the spiritual strongholds in a community.

- **Tongues:** is Spirit-inspired speaking in which the conscious mind plays no direct part. It is the speaking of a language (whether a known language or angelic) which has never been learned by the speaker. Tongues is used for the strengthening of our spirit in our own private prayer time. It is also used in First Church gatherings.

- **Interpretation of tongues:** is the companion gift to tongues. It is the God-given inspiration to interpret the tongue that has just been spoken (either by that person or someone else in the gathering) and to speak it in the language of the listeners, giving them the dynamic equivalent of that which was just spoken.

When spiritual gifts are in operation in any gathering, they are accompanied by a palpable increase in corporate awareness of the near and powerful presence of the Holy Spirit. For over forty years, I have witnessed this phenomenon more times than I could ever remember. In this atmosphere of spiritual gifts, I have seen men and women healed and delivered; I have seen unbelievers quite literally fall to the floor in repentance; I have seen churches, small groups and First Churches transformed.

Indeed, I have witnessed greater and more profound transformation happen in just moments of such powerful manifestations of the Holy Spirit than I could see in months or years of teaching. This is why the apostles reminded the early church again and again that they are to hold on to the reality of "walking in the Spirit".

When a First Church or small group flows in spiritual gifts as a lifestyle, they become like a lighthouse in the community. Everywhere, there are men and women longing for deep spiritual connection. Many need to be healed; others need the building up, encouragement and comfort that a prophetic word supplies. Regardless of the need, where spiritual gifts are operating, no matter their background, people recognize that God is present, and it is His presence that draws men, women and children to Himself. Therefore, gatherings that are committed to a lifestyle of exercising spiritual gifts, become the salt and light that Jesus declared we were created to be.

We have an enemy, an adversary, who is constantly pushing against us. One of the principal ways he does this is by trying to draw our eyes away from what the Spirit of God is doing so that we begin to live limited by our natural thinking and perceptions. We are in a continual battle not to be "conformed by the things of this world" (Ro 12:1) which is under the steady influence of the enemy and the powers that serve his purposes. That is why Paul wrote to the Galatians,

> *"After starting your Christian lives in the Spirit, why are you now trying to become perfect by your own*

human effort?"

(Gal 3:3 NLT)

With the enemy pushing against us, it is all too easy in our gatherings to gradually move away from the spontaneous and surprising move of the Holy Spirit, toward the predictability of our planned and structured meetings.

The gifts of the Spirit release His great purposes in our midst whenever we make room for them. As Paul told the Corinthians:

> *"Pursue love and desire spiritual gifts, and above all that you may prophesy."*

(1 Cor 14:1 CSB)

All of the gifts of the Spirit are precious, but there is something unique about prophecy. Not only are the secrets of people's hearts revealed, leading them to repentance, prophecy seems to have a quality about it that uniquely unlocks the purposes of God. My own life's journey has, on many occasions, been directed and adjusted through receiving prophetic words. This has included selling everything and moving with my family across the continent four different times. In every instance, we moved into a new and larger sphere of fruitfulness. None of these moves would have happened without the Lord specifically speaking to us through the gift of prophecy. The prophetic word itself not only reveals God's will in a situation, it carries the power of God to fulfill that which is declared.

For many who have come from a Pentecostal or charismatic

> When a First Church flows in spiritual gifts, it is living in the reality of "heaven now"; this is what everyone was made for.

tradition, the gift of prophecy has often come in a particular (and often intimidating) package. In this model, prophecies often begin with "Thus sayeth the Lord!" and are often expressed in a rather strange tone of voice, often expressed in King James English. Not only is this kind of prophetic expression rather off-putting to visitors, it can create an unspoken standard for the other First Church members. Let me emphasize what I have already written: prophecy is simply listening to what the Lord is saying and then speaking that out. Its purpose is to build up, encourage and comfort. None of that requires a special kind of "delivery".

Randeep told me the following example of how a prophetic word spoken in a First Church, when received, unlocked a great move of God:

> "One day while our house church was gathered, a young man came in for the first time. I didn't know who this man was, but suddenly, the Spirit of God told me that He was going to start a mighty move through this young man. When I spoke the prophetic word, he said to me, 'How can this be?' This was because he was totally backslidden. Though once he had attended church, he had felt hurt by several different churches. As a result, he felt great bitterness toward the church. Right then, God revealed that this young man needed to forgive all

the churches that had hurt him. The house church helped him to pray through this and come to the place of truly forgiving everyone.

After this, he went to another city and planted a house church. Today, this whole area is flooded with house churches. This has all happened because of the prophecy that he received in a house church."

When the person of peace witnesses and experiences spiritual gifts from his or her first encounter with the Gospel, these gifts are immediately established as normative. Therefore, not only do they quickly become what he expects, spiritual gifts are what he or she will operate in from the very first day, and this is what will be passed on to others.

When a First Church flows in spiritual gifts, it is living in the reality of "heaven now"; this is what everyone was made for. Therefore, a group that freely moves in the Holy Spirit is attractive to newcomers who instinctively feel a sense of homecoming, a deep awareness of discovering something that was missing in their lives. This longing, though hard to express, is universal. C.S. Lewis addresses this in *The Weight of Glory*:

"If we are made for heaven, the desire for our proper place will be already in us... we remain conscious of a desire which no natural happiness will satisfy." [1]

---

1 C.S. Lewis, *The Weight of Glory* (San Francisco: Harper Collins, 1976), 29,32.

"[O]ur longing to be reunited with something in the universe from which we now feel cut off, to be on the inside of some door which we have always seen from the outside, is no mere neurotic fancy, but the truest index of our real situation...We want something else which can hardly be put into words—to be united with the beauty we see, to pass into it, to receive it into ourselves, to bathe in it, to become part of it."[2]

I will always remember the first time I came into a place where men and women were worshiping the Lord and flowing in the gifts of the Holy Spirit. I was a totally unchurched man, so this was all new to me. Rather than feeling uncomfortable or embarrassed, what I will always remember is the profound sense that I was finally home. This is the homecoming for which everyone longs and, indeed, was created for. Like the family life of true community, the presence of God and the flowing of His spiritual gifts are why, in the early church and in our time, "the Lord added daily to their number".

"Trailing clouds of glory do we come
From God, who is our home."[3]

PUTTING IT INTO PRACTICE

1. Whenever you come together, *expect* the Lord to move (Mt 18:20). The Lord blesses our faith and expectation.

---

2 Ibid, 42

3 William Wordsworth, *Ode: Intimations of Immortality*

2. Always specifically invite the Holy Spirit to move in your midst, then wait for His presence to be felt.

3. Discuss the various spiritual gifts listed in 1 Cor. 12 and 14. (There are other lists elsewhere, for example Ro 12:6-8 and Eph 4:11.)

    • After you have discussed a specific spiritual gift, *put what you have learned into practice.* Immediately take time for each member to step out.

    • Make sure that you all agree that it is okay for someone to make a mistake. This is vital in order to have a safe atmosphere.

    • Sometimes it is easier to break into smaller groups of 4 or 5.

4. Remember, the Kingdom of God is in the Holy Spirit (Ro 14:17). The enemy knows that a First Church or small group that is regularly operating in spiritual gifts is powerful. Therefore he will try to intimidate or distract.

    • Don't lose focus, or drift away from this. Always move in spiritual gifts whenever you gather.

    • By doing this, you are coming in the opposite spirit and thereby disempowering the enemy. Spiritual gifts are powerful warfare.

12

Hospitality: The Missing Missional Ingredient

"Do not neglect hospitality, because through it some have entertained angels without knowing it."

Hebrews 13:2

In 2013, I traveled to India to observe the exploding First Church movement that I had heard and read about. Beside the gatherings themselves, that I have written about in the previous chapters, there was an atmosphere, an ethos, in the various houses where I stayed that was altogether new to me. Near the end of my journey, I stayed in Randeep and Anu's home for four or five days. This was my first time meeting them. Their house was always full of people, mostly young adults. I would go to bed at night to the sound of worship, a cricket game on the television, people praying, or others cooking in the kitchen. On the mornings that I was first up, I would see people sleeping all over the floor. This happened every day. Finally, after the third day, I asked Anu if it was always like this. I will never forget her reply. She looked at me quizzically and said, "Of course. This is the church."

"This is the church." These words sent me back to reading about the early church, where the believers continuously gathered and ate in homes as, daily, the Lord added to their number. This was a time when there were no church buildings, and evangelistic meetings were unheard of, yet, for 300 years the church grew at a spectacular rate. By 300 A.D., the church numbered *six million*, making up ten percent of the population of the Roman empire.[1] Historical sources tell us that the early church was marked by three things: healing and miracles; care for the poor and the outcast; and hospitality.

As I have met with churches and small groups of many varieties in a number of nations, I have come to the conclusion that (to quote Jesus in Luke 18:22), "there is still one thing you lack"—hospitality. This may be the single biggest key to turning our churches outward, to shift them from being exclusive to inclusive. I can almost hear the protests: "But we have friends from the church over all the time, and we host our small group's Christmas potluck almost every year!" Clearly that is a good thing; no one should say otherwise. But it leads us to a confusion of terms that needs to be clarified.

---

1 https://www.thegospelcoalition.org/blogs/justin-taylor/early-church-growth/

HOSPITALITY IN THE EARLY CHURCH

Since about 500 AD, two "church" words have been used almost interchangeably: *fellowship and hospitality*. However, during the first 300 years of the church, these words expressed two very different meanings. Fellowship, or *koinonia*, meant "communion" and described the life of the believers together, including the idea of sharing in common. Paul uses the term nine times in his letters. Acts 2:42-47 is a beautiful description of Biblical fellowship where the believers shared their lives with one another.

For the early church, hospitality, on the other hand, was something quite different. The New Testament word for hospitality, *philoxenia*, literally means love of strangers. Paul, Peter, and the writer to the Hebrews all urged their listeners to reach out beyond their usual circle, and beyond the church, to include other people.

From the earliest days of the Bible, hospitality was central to life and highly valued. Abraham's great encounter with the Lord in Genesis 18 began with him taking the initiative to invite the three men (actually the Lord and two angels) to stop for dinner. This sets the pattern throughout the Old Testament where so many significant events happened around the table. This pattern carries on in the Gospels, where we see Jesus as either guest or host. Even a cursory reading of the Gospels reveals how meals were so central to Jesus' ministry, for example at Matthew's house, at Simon's home in Bethany and at the Last Supper. It is important to the structure of John's Gospel that the first miracle took place at a wedding feast, and that the final exchange with the disciples in chapter 21 took place over breakfast.

The New Testament church continued with the centrality of the shared meal. In many ways, the early church lived as an extended family. This provided a natural and effective way of expressing hospitality to "outsiders" that reflected the gracious and hospitable character of God.[2] From the beginning, this kind of hospitality set the church apart from the surrounding society. Conventionally in the Roman world, hospitality was for family, friends and influential people. Hospitality was practiced strategically, whether to enhance one's social standing or to maintain harmonious relationships. However, for the early church, hospitality was the practical expression of God's love for people.

> To cities filled with the homeless, impoverished, and strangers, Christians offered an immediate basis for attachments. To cities filled with orphans and widows, Christians provided a new and expanded sense of family.[3]

Hospitality was a key that set the early church apart from the surrounding culture. Perhaps surprisingly, it was their inclusiveness and care for the disenfranchised that made the church so attractive. The early church grew, in the midst of

---

2 Christina Pohl *Making Room* (Grand Rapids, MI: Wm. Eerdman Pub. 1999), p 42.

3 ,https://place.asburyseminary.edu/cgi/viewcontent.cgi?article=1074&context=firstfruitspapers p. 11

persecution and hardship, at a rate of 40% every decade for the first three hundred years. Historians from a wide variety of viewpoints agree that one of the most important contributing factors was the church's unwavering lifestyle of hospitality. In this, the church was talking Jesus' words literally:

"Go quickly into the streets and alleys of the town and invite the crippled, the lame, and the blind."

(Lu 14:21 NLT)

HOSPITALITY IN THE NEW COMMUNITY

Has there ever been a better time to re-discover Biblical hospitality than in the 21st century? So many factors have collided in our post-modern world to create a perfect storm of isolation. North Americans move on average every 3½ years. Technology has vastly reduced face-to-face human contact; in everything from online shopping and banking to the steady increase of e-communities, no personal interaction is needed in order to belong. Alongside this is the rise in violent crime and the marginalization of ethnic groups, and the breakdown of the family unit. The result is an absence of meaningful, authentic community. Most of us live in neighborhoods where people simply do not know each other.

However, the Creator is expressed in the community of the Trinity; His relational stamp is upon all that He has made. Remember, every person was created with two great needs: security and significance. But with increased societal isolation, the deep need for connection, though perhaps suppressed, will not go away. We were simply made for one another. Yet, as Winfield Bevins has noted in *Ever Ancient, Ever New*,

> Sadly, many contemporary Christians and churches have lost touch with the biblical importance of extending hospitality to strangers.[4]

Biblical hospitality, the kind of hospitality written about in the New Testament, goes beyond our preferences and desire for social interaction; rather, it is a lifestyle that we embrace because of devotion to Jesus and love for people. This kind of hospitality reaches out beyond our Christian friends and makes our homes available to others as oases of love and acceptance. *This* is what brings recovery and healing to people and sets our homes as the 'city on a hill' that Jesus called us to be. New Testament hospitality does not happen for an hour or two a week; it is a lifestyle of openness and availability that flows from a deep conviction that because we love God, therefore we actively and inclusively love people.

In a number of New Testament translations, Paul's words to the Roman church are recorded as, "practice hospitality" (12:13); he actually said *pursue* hospitality. This speaks of being proactive, of following the example of the seeking and inviting King, rather than waiting for our neighbors to reach out to us, or waiting for "just the right time". This takes us back to the imperative of the Great Commission: it is a "go"

---

4 Winfield Beven *Ever Ancient, Ever New* (Grand Rapids, MI: Zondervan Pub, 2019) p. 124

gospel. Jesus was always missional and He called the church to be a missional church. Pursuing hospitality was so important to the early church that Paul made it a requirement for leadership (1 Tim 3:2; Titus 1:8). This wasn't a suggestion; Paul made hospitality an imperative for anyone in leadership. Paul knew that people follow the example of elders and deacons.

Peter was being realistic when he wrote, "Offer hospitality to one another without complaint." (1 Pet 4:9). Often, being hospitable means sacrificing our comfort and convenience. Peter knew that these are very real. There are times when we need to count the cost, as we make our homes places of refuge and encouragement for others. The single most repeated saying of Jesus was, "Whoever seeks to save his life will lose it, but whoever loses his life for My sake will find it." (Mt 16:25). Choosing a lifestyle of hospitality makes this verse very practical. But we do it for the sake of Jesus and the Gospel. We tangibly love God and love our neighbor.

> Biblical hospitality goes far beyond friendliness; it relects life as God intended it to be: radically inclusive, with the vibrant life of the Trinity flowing in our midst. Such hospitality doesn't invite someone to be included into a meeting; it is an invitation into a family.

In Hebrews 13:2 we read, "Do not neglect to show hospitality to strangers, for by doing that some have entertained angels without knowing it". The key word for me is *stranger*, because of the Lord's last teaching before His arrest:

"I was hungry and you gave Me something to eat, I was thirsty and you gave me something to drink, I was a stranger and you invited me in"

(Mt 25:35 NIV)

When we reach out to the stranger, we are reaching out to Jesus. When we love the stranger, we are loving Jesus. Biblical hospitality is powerful on many levels.

Hospitality makes practical the inclusion that we find in the life and teaching of Jesus. No one lived as inclusive a life as Jesus; therefore, the gospel is always inclusive. This reflects the family values that Jesus gave to His followers when He said,

"Whoever does the will of My Father in heaven, that person is My brother and sister and mother."

(Mt 12:50 CSB)

Biblical hospitality goes far beyond friendliness; it reflects life as God intended it to be: radically inclusive, with the vibrant life of the Trinity flowing in our midst. Such hospitality doesn't invite someone to be included into a meeting; it is an invitation into a family. This gift of welcome shares both what we have and who we are; it is both given and received. More than opening our door, to welcome means to give space to someone in our hearts and lives. There is an openness and even vulnerability that comes with true welcome.

Hospitality is, at its heart, a visible demonstration of the Gospel. It shows what is possible when people determine to live inclusively and to reach out to one another. This is the life for which we were created. Remember: *everyone* was made for relationship, for community. When we choose hospitality, we are moving in the footsteps of Jesus and in the rhythm of His cosmos. That is why for years, I have watched hospitality come with often surprising favor. Paul said that we "carry with us everywhere the fragrance of Christ" (2 Cor 2:14). There is a supernatural attractiveness that is released through welcome. It changes the atmosphere. In a day when our western churches are struggling to grow (or hold onto the members they have), when so much energy is going into attracting new people and then holding on to them, I am convinced that the better, and much more effective way, is a very ancient one: the gift of hospitality.

BELONGING COMES BEFORE BELIEVING

Practicing corporate hospitality, whether in our home groups, Bible studies or First Churches, will quickly lead us to a new paradigm: *belonging comes before believing*. This is a major shift from how we have done church. Essentially, we have presented a message that says, "If you will pray a prayer to receive Jesus, then you can be one of us". However, the early church model, and what I have witnessed repeatedly where the First Church movement is growing so rapidly, is a very different approach. It welcomes all unconditionally, confident that simply by being with this Christ-infused family, before long the newcomer will fall in love with the One that the family loves. Almost no one that I meet in the First Church movement can tell me when they prayed "the sinner's prayer" (which is nowhere to be found in the Bible). They simply, step by step, fall in love with Jesus as they experience Him in the midst of this new family.

This was the pattern the first century believers had learned from Jesus who invited people to follow Him. No strings. When asked where He was staying, He simply replied, "Come and you will see" (Jn 1:39). Repeatedly, Jesus invited people to follow Him and by doing so, to become part of a growing company of people. He told no one that they had to believe or do anything before they could come. His whole life said, "You come too. Of course, you are included." Radical hospitality.

Recently, I asked Randeep, in light of having over 800,000 disciples in almost 20,000 First Churches how many people drift away each year. At first, he didn't understand the question. After I re-phrased it, Randeep smiled at me and said, "None". "How can that be?" I replied incredulously. I will always remember his answer: People never leave their families.

People never leave their families. This is vital for us to understand. We work so hard to convince people to join our meetings. But God never created us for meetings; He created us for family. If we really understand this, it will change the way we do church, whether it is a First Church model or a small group.

EMBRACING CHANGE

When we commit to embracing hospitality, we are immediately stretched and challenged. For most of us, it means a conscious shift, a change in our priorities and schedules that confront our comfort, convenience, and preferences. Hospitality disturbs our routines and pushes our boundaries, but it is when we leave the familiar that we so often find Jesus waiting there for us. Some of the resistance and reluctance we feel is, frankly, spiritual warfare. Our enemy knows how powerful it is when we move in the rhythm of the Lord's hospitality, so he often tries to fill our minds with thoughts of being too busy or tired, or fear of having our hospitality rejected. Our flesh may resist, but our spirit responds to the Lord's prompting. That is why Peter admonished the church to be hospitable without grumbling. Peter was a realist. As I wrote earlier, the single most repeated saying of Jesus was, *"Whoever seeks to save his life will lose it, but whoever loses his life for My sake will find it."* Choosing a lifestyle of hospitality makes this verse very practical.

Hospitality is a powerful way of responding to Jesus' invitation to "Follow Me." Jesus is passionate about people. He is the One who constantly sought people out—and He hasn't changed. We pursue hospitality for the sake of Jesus and the gospel. We choose to love our neighbor. To make following Jesus real and not some kind of idealism, something is always required: movement. Jesus is on the move, and He invites us to move with Him. But here is the truth that causes us to move from theory to practice: we can't go somewhere unless we leave somewhere. (I wrote this in an earlier chapter, but it is so fundamental that it bears repeating.) Following Jesus will always mean changing how we do things.

ATTENTIVENESS

Hospitality is more than offering food and drink; it is offering the gift of attentiveness. One of the greatest acts of love and care is the gift of listening. In our post-modern world filled with a cacophony of words and with information overload, to simply give someone our full attention, striving to really listen to what they are saying, has a powerful impact. When we give the gift of our attention to people, we are expressing their value—both to us and to the Lord. Listening communicates that they have found with us a place of peace, acceptance and safety.

THE SACREDNESS OF EATING TOGETHER

Earlier, I wrote how important it is to gather around the table for a corporate meal. Beginning in the kitchen at 6 pm instead of in the living room at 7:30 was one of the most profound discoveries I have ever made about the dynamics of small group gatherings.

In any culture, one of the most powerful expressions of welcome that can be offered is the invitation to eat together. To invite someone to share at our dinner table is to invite them into an important part of our lives. It expresses not only interest, but inclusion. The table is, perhaps more than anywhere else, the place where life happens, as the simple exchange of the day's events often opens the door to the convictions, observations, concerns, hopes and dreams that we carry in our hearts. When our sons still lived at home, the supper table was the focal point of our family life together. For years, I watched whenever one of us invited someone to join us for dinner how they would relax, open up and participate in the energy and love that flowed around the table.

In eating together, I often think of Jesus' promise: "Where two or three are gathered in My name, there I am among them" (Mt 18:20 ESV). There really is something sacred about eating together. In one sense, whenever we gather to eat it is a prophetic act, pointing to the Lamb's Feast of Revelation 19.

BE INTENTIONAL

Remember that Paul said, "Pursue hospitality"(Ro 12:13). This calls for us to be intentional and to be proactive. A major result of my visits to India to observe so many First Churches and their daily practice of hospitality, was to become more deliberate at home. Instead of waiting for opportunities to be hospitable, I began to facilitate them. Like most of us western Christians, virtually all of my significant relationships were with other believers. Instead of beating myself up about this, I began to specifically reach out to people outside of my comfort zone.

Like many of you, I have spent a reasonable amount of time praying for my neighbors, asking God to move on our street. Prayer walking our streets like this is good; we are inviting the Holy Spirit to go before us. But after I returned from India,

I realized that two years of praying had not opened up the homes on my street to the Gospel. So, I started knocking on the doors of my neighbors and simply inviting them to come over for coffee or a meal. I know, this isn't rocket science. But when I started this simple proactive obedience, I discovered something. My neighbors (without exception) said, "Yes, we'd love to come over." And this has continued for many years now. When we moved to other cities, once again, we started inviting the neighbors over for a meal. Again, no one ever refused. We have made new friends and we have had many opportunities to pray for and with them. Early on, we noticed something: when there was a problem in their lives, often our neighbors would drop by to talk. Why? Because like you, we carry with us the fragrance of Christ. Because of this supernatural fragrance, when our neighbors come into our homes, they experience peace and life. We don't have to try to be Christians: we already are. That's why Jesus said, "You *are* the salt of the earth and the light of the world"—not you *should* be.

I encourage you to put this into practice. There is nothing to wait for. Step out your front door, walk to a neighbor's that you don't really know, knock on their door and simply invite them to come over later in the week. Then watch what Jesus does. And when they come, relax. Don't try to work the conversation around to talking about the Lord. Don't try to pray for them. Just wait. Don't answer questions that they are not asking. Simply practice hospitality. Make a new friend, because friendship is the bridge that we eventually build discipleship upon. Sometimes it surprises us how quickly that happens; sometimes we have to wait. And while we wait, be attentive; love them; be a friend.

Paul reminds us that "we have this treasure in earthen vessels" (2 Cor 4:7). Following Jesus means that in spite of our weaknesses, our fear of the unfamiliar, our failings and weaknesses, still our eyes are fixed on Him and we go where he goes—and He always goes to people. In pursuing Biblical hospitality, we are willing to lose the preferences and conveniences of our lives in order to find them in a whole new (and often unfamiliar) way. As we follow the seeking, inviting, inclusive Jesus, we choose to join the early church—and the explosive church of the developing world—and to go to the poor, the isolated, our neighbors and co-workers. We choose to invite them into our homes and our lives. We choose to embrace, include, and share life. This is the rhythm of the One who came for the whole world.

They ate together in their homes, happy to share their food with joyful hearts. They praised God and were liked by all the people. Every day the Lord added those who were being saved to the group of believers.

(Acts 2:46-47 NCV)

13

What to Teach a Disciple

"And the things you have heard me say in the presence of many witnesses entrust to reliable people who will also be qualified to teach others."

2 Timothy 2:2

We have established that Jesus gave us, the church, a central command: "Go and make disciples." We have also looked at how small group structures, especially First Churches, are an ideal way to facilitate obedience to that command. Earlier, in chapter seven, we learned how in the early church, the worship service was foundational in making disciples, teaching them how to pray, worship, understand scripture, and discern Christ's presence during the Lord's Supper. However, we must not overlook the way in which new disciples were formed through personal time with more mature disciples. Now it is time to get practical. *How* exactly, do we make disciples?

As always, methods must remain secondary to our objective. The key is always understanding the goal and the principles that help us reach that goal. One of the weaknesses of our western way of thinking is that we have a great tendency to find an existing strategy and then simply copy its methodology. Over the past 30 years I have watched as North American pastors (including me) found out what was working elsewhere and then sought to copy it. I spent several years implementing the Cell Church method out of Singapore, only to find that there were some great principles, but it couldn't (and probably shouldn't) be copied in our culture. Similarly, many of my pastor friends embraced a variation, the G-12 method that had been so successful in South America, only to discover that it didn't produce anywhere near the same results in North America.

It is therefore with caution that I share some fairly concrete principles; it is vital that we understand the "why" more than the "what" of these concepts. However, I have always found it helpful to have a track to run on.

Disciples do what Jesus did; they go where He went—often to the people that others bypassed or didn't see at all. This is, in large part, what it means to follow Jesus. If we are going to follow Him, then we must learn to hear Him. Jesus modeled this for us in His walk:

> *"I tell you the truth, the Son can do nothing by himself. He does only what he sees the Father doing. Whatever the Father does, the Son also does."*
>
> *(Jn 5:19 NLT)*

"I can do nothing on my own. As I hear, I judge; and my judgement is just, because I seek to do not my own will but the will of him who sent me."

(Jn 5:30 NRSV)

Jesus was able to do only what the Father did and said because He had learned to *hear and recognize* the Father's voice and to *perceive* what the Father was doing. I have long been convinced that Jesus learned this through a lifelong pattern of stepping away from the pull of this world in order to spend time with the Father in prayer. The disciples recognized the centrality and power of this in His life, to the extent that they specifically asked Jesus to teach them to pray like He did.

Much of what I am writing in this chapter has come from both long talks with some of my friends in the Indian house church movement, and as a result of observing how they are making effective disciples. I want to thank Anuroop Swamy and Randeep Mathews especially for all that you have taught and modeled. The guidelines for making disciples presented in this chapter come directly from what Anuroop taught me.

In Paul's final letter, Second Timothy, written while he was alone in prison, he exhorted Timothy:

"You have heard me teach things that have been confirmed by many reliable witnesses. Now teach these truths to other trustworthy people who will be able to pass them on to others."

(2 Ti 2:2 NLT)

In this one statement lie the seeds of exponential growth, of ongoing multiplication, of empowering lives that will empower others, and so on, and so on. One of the great strengths of First Churches is that they are built upon discipleship; from the first day someone comes in, he or she begins to be discipled, even before they turn to Christ. Remember, when I referenced the 800,000+ disciples in Randeep's house church network, they are only counted if they have been baptized in water and are truly being discipled in a house church. Hands raised in a large meeting are not counted.

Looking at this passage, it is important that we focus on "these truths." What exactly are disciples taught?

There are five foundational values that give us the direction and framework for making disciples. The key is not intellectual agreement with these values; rather, we pursue ways to concretely apply them in the lives of those we disciple.

1. *Love God with your whole heart, soul and mind.* Lead the disciple into a radical new life, built around loving God in every area.

2. *Love your neighbor.* When we love God, we will love people. One of the greatest ways we love God is by loving those around us. Moreover, He will send us specific people—our neighbor—to very intentionally love. This expands loving God beyond our personal prayer time with Him, sending us out to love Him through our neighbor.

3. *When we love our neighbor, we will disciple Him.* The overarching goal of discipleship is to make them like Jesus, who always reached out to the lost sheep. Therefore, if I love my neighbor, I will make him a disciple.

4. *Where we make disciples is where we plant a church.* Our goal is to make disciples who in turn make disciples. It is not to organize people into a church. Disciple-making is much more organic. As we gather with disciples, the Holy Spirit is in our midst. His presence will draw more people. Disciples who understand the Great Commission will be intentional about loving their neighbors and making disciples. The result: a church is formed by the Lord, not our church growth strategies.

5. *Where a church is planted, God's Kingdom is established.* The church lives in the reality of Heaven now—righteousness, peace and joy in the power of the Holy Spirit. (Ro 14:17)

Built upon these foundational values, we instruct the new disciples in the following six key truths:

WATER BAPTISM

Upon turning his or her life to Christ, the first truth is to be baptized in water. There is no delaying this step. It is vital that the new disciple enters into the spiritual power that comes in water baptism. I recall listening to Anuroop explain baptism to a group of curious Canadians a few years ago. He told them how he establishes the importance of the commitment of baptism. He will agree to meet the new disciple at a public body of water, at a given time on that same day. If the disciple comes alone, Anuroop tells him, "I'm confused. You don't have anyone with you to witness your baptism. You need to go back and get some people to witness your baptism before I can baptize you." Not once has anyone failed to return, usually with several friends and family members. (New disciples have been known to bring as many as seven others with them, many of whom gave their lives to Christ.)

EMPOWERED BY THE HOLY SPIRIT

Either during or following water baptism, we pray for the new believer to be baptized in the Spirit. (This is a term still common in the developing world, perhaps less so these days in the West. But whatever the terminology, it refers to a specific empowering and filling by the Holy Spirit.) It is so important from the beginning that new disciples both understand and experience an empowered walk with the Triune God. This infilling usually comes as a result of us laying hands on the disciple, releasing an impartation of the Holy Spirit. This was a central apostolic activity in the early church. Laying hands upon people and praying for impartation was standard practice.

Hebrews 6:1-2 lists the basic teachings for new believers:

"Therefore let us leave the elementary teachings about

Christ and go on to maturity, not laying again the foundation of repentance from acts that lead to death, and of faith in God, instruction about baptisms, the laying on of hands, the resurrection of the dead, and eternal judgment." (NIV)

Laying hands upon someone for anointing is basic to Christian life and should be part of our "elementary teachings" for new believers. It is done for several purposes:

- To receive the empowering of the Holy Spirit.

"The Holy Spirit had not yet come upon any of them...Then Peter and John laid their hands upon these believers, and they received the Holy Spirit."
(Acts 8:16-17 NLT)

"When Paul placed his hands on them, the Holy Spirit came on them, and they spoke in tongues and prophesied."
(Acts 19:6 NIV)

- To commission. In Acts 13, Paul and Barnabas were commissioned to go out to the Gentiles through the laying on of hands by the Antioch leaders. Paul did the same with Timothy. (1Ti 4:14)

LISTENING TO JESUS

From the first day, the disciple is taught to recognize the voice

Becoming a disciple of Jesus is so much more than believing points of doctrine, or even church attendance. Being a disciple means to follow Him; and following Him means we go where He is going and do what He is doing.

of Jesus. In fact, because He is everywhere at all times, people can hear from Jesus even before they turn to Him. He has no limits. I have found the same thing with healing. On a number of occasions, I have had not-yet-believers lay hands on the sick and pray for them. They are often surprised when the person they prayed for is healed; more importantly, in an instant they are confronted with the reality of Jesus and His power. It is the same with hearing His voice. From the beginning, it is vital that new disciples understand that Jesus is always speaking and that they can hear him. After all, Jesus said, "My sheep hear my voice" (Jn 10:27). On the day of Pentecost, when Peter addressed the crowd to explain what was happening, he quoted the prophet Joel:

> *"And it will be in the last days, says God,*
> *that I will pour out My Spirit on all humanity;*
> *then your sons and your daughters will prophesy*
> *your young men will see visions*
> *and your old men will dream dreams."*
> *(Acts 2:17 CSB)*

Note: *all* humanity. The Lord often reveals Himself through these manifestations of His Spirit; discipleship begins with teaching people to be attentive. Joel declares that in this age of the Spirit (the last days), people will prophesy. To de-mystify this, prophecy in this Age simply means to hear what the Lord is saying, or showing in a mental image, and then speaking that out. It is done simply and humbly, recognizing that for our entire lives we are learning to hear more clearly and so we will not always get it right. The point is to experience the reality that Jesus speaks to us personally. For years, I have witnessed Him speaking and healing with both believers and unbelievers; this includes Hindus and Muslims. In an instant, Christ becomes a reality, not a theology.

When, from the beginning, people understand at a personal level that Jesus speaks, and that He speaks specifically to them, their relationship with Him is both real and intimate. They enter experientially into a love affair with the living God. This is the true foundation of every authentic relationship.

DECISION MAKING

Becoming a disciple of Jesus is so much more than believing points of doctrine, or even faithful church attendance. Being a disciple means to follow Him; and following Him means we go where He is going and to do what He is doing (Jn 5:19; 12:26). One of the greatest watersheds of discipleship is moving from a self-centered life to a Christ-centered one. Surely, this is what Jesus meant when He said we must lose our lives in order to truly find them. Such a shift affects everything–our priorities, our values, and our goals. A disciple progressively learns to join Jesus in his Garden prayer: "not my will, but yours be done."

A key to making this real in the new disciple's life, is to teach him or her to go through each day conversationally with Jesus. Quickly we discover that He cares about the details of our lives. One of the big challenges in my life was (and still is) learning that what He has for me on any given day was often different than what I had planned on. For all of my adult life, I have begun the day by writing a "to do" list, based on what I think are the most important things to accomplish. But the Lord has encounters waiting for us every day, if we will just learn to slow down and listen. If we develop a lifestyle of talking with (and listening to) Jesus throughout the day, we will begin to learn to really follow Him in what He is up to.

THE SCRIPTURES

From the beginning, teach new disciples to read the scriptures. Of course, there are seemingly endless approaches to this. Here are a few guidelines:

- Begin with the New Testament. Teach them to read a chapter from the Gospels every day. This has been my pattern for over thirty years. For me, daily time in the Gospels is a vital part of following Jesus. At the same time, begin in Acts and work through the rest of the New Testament. Acts gives a wonderful context for how the early church lived and grew.

- The early fathers and mothers of the church taught a method of slow reading called *Lectio Divina*. While reading, note what verses stand out; these are likely the ones that the Holy Spirit is highlighting. Read these few verses very slowly. Think about them, then turn them into a prayer. Following this, simply be still and let the Lord speak. This is a wonderful way, from the beginning, for a disciple to learn the spiritual discipline of attentiveness. It also helps him or her to understand that the Bible is a love letter from the Lord that leads us to His heart, not an owner's manual with principles that must be learned.

- After some time, encourage the disciple to begin reading the Old Testament, beginning in Genesis and the Psalms, reading a chapter from each. Over time, the disciple can progress from these two starting points. It will take about one year to read the entire Old Testament.

- Years ago, as a new disciple, I was taught to journal what the Lord was speaking to me through the scriptures. This included observations, impressions from the Lord, and questions.

- Teach them from the scriptures, both Old and New Testament, about Jesus. He is the beginning and end of everything. The apostles taught Jesus. The early church proclaimed Jesus. Teach them about Jesus.

- No matter which approach is taken, it is important that we regularly interact with the disciple as he or she is learning about the Bible. Dialogue is probably the most effective teaching method of all. As a teacher, my favorite format is *question and answer*. That way, I know what the disciple is wrestling with, or is interested in. Also, it lets me know what needs clarification.

From the beginning, we want to encourage a love for the scriptures, for they reveal Jesus Christ, "full of grace and truth."

TEACH THEM TO MAKE DISCIPLES

Remember the Great Commission: disciples make disciples. One of the biggest surprises I had when first encountering the disciple-making movement in India, was how *quickly* new believers were encouraged to themselves make disciples. Coming from my western church paradigm, it was shocking (not too strong a word) to see people who had turned to Christ only a few days earlier now not only evangelizing, but actually discipling others. The house churches do not accomplish this through programs but through instilling principles and values from the very beginning. Second Timothy 2:2 is the core principle. As the new disciple is learning and being transformed, he or she immediately begins to teach these things to an even newer (or not-yet) believer.

Teaching new believers to make disciples begins with the foundation of the Great Commandment:

"He said to them, 'Love the Lord your God with all your

heart, with all your soul, and with all your mind. This is
the greatest and most important command. The second
is like it: love your neighbor as yourself. All the Law
and the Prophets depend on these two commands.'"

(Mt 22:37-40 NLT)

These are two equally important commands ("the second is like it")—love God; love people. Love for God cannot, therefore, be greater than love for our neighbor. In fact, we legitimize our love for God through our demonstration of love for people. If we will be true to this great command, we cannot love people casually or half-heartedly; instead, we must love them with our whole attention (heart, soul and mind). With this command, Jesus is challenging exclusive relationships. The One who always invited everyone, including the socially unattractive, calls us to live the same way. How do we make this practical?

This takes us back to the issue of being attentive to what Jesus is saying and doing. He always reached beyond the borders of people's expectations, and He is still doing this today. So, we start with asking Him who He is leading us to. Sometimes we get a definite impression of a particular person or family, but often He shows us this as we go through our day. This is especially true if we live intentionally, determined to express friendship to all we meet. Assume Jesus is always on the move and He is inviting us along.

We can answer the question of how we are to love our neighbor with one question: How can I bring this person to Christ? This question helps to direct all our intentions toward that person.

Our motive must never be a sense of achievement or conquest for the Lord. No, as the greatest act of care we can give, we are to introduce them to the love, grace, forgiveness and beauty of the One who has captured our heart. The journey to Jesus may be long or short, but it is always full of purpose, compassion and great love.

There is another powerful component to loving our neighbor: the family of God. In the earlier chapter on hospitality, I wrote about an early church principle that I see lived out where the church is growing so explosively in the developing world—*belonging comes before believing*. When, as part of loving our neighbor, we introduce them to some of our friends, this opens up a whole new dimension. Inclusion is powerful simply because it demonstrates love and acceptance. But there is a whole other level. Jesus said that wherever two or three come together, He is in their midst. Many times, I have seen a newcomer impacted by the presence of the Lord (often without even knowing what that Presence is) and open his or her heart to Jesus without persuasion or even discussion. As the Apostle Paul wrote to the church in Corinth, when the newcomer witnesses the manifestations of the Lord's presence, when spiritual gifts like prophecy and healing are flowing in a gathering, he recognizes that God is in their midst (1 Cor 14:24). At other times, the newcomer, presented with being included into the lives of new friends, simply falls in love with the people and then, sometime later, falls in love with the One that these friends love.

The First Church (or any kind of intentional, missional small group) is the ideal setting for discipleship to take place. It is in the gathering where Jesus is building His church (Mt 16:18). He builds it *in and through* us as we share our daily struggles and victories, the joy and the pain going on in our lives, and as we are encouraged and comforted by one another and His Spirit. These gatherings are filled with teachable moments as spiritual and lifestyle issues arise. In His presence we learn to pray, to heal in His name, and to celebrate His transformational work in our lives.

———————

Standing before the religious leaders of Judea, Peter declared that "there is no other name by which we can be saved" (Acts 4:12). Salvation touches every area of life. There isn't spiritual and natural: Jesus came to rescue and transform all parts of our lives. In my discussions with my friend Anuroop about how he makes disciples, I was surprised how concrete his approach is. He described five distinct areas that he addresses in the lives of disciples. Anuroop is convinced that each of these areas is needed in order to experience Christ's salvation.

1. *Redeem the soul.* Share the love of Jesus in the context of living life with our neighbors. Once they turn to Him (repentance), immediately lead them to water baptism and Holy Spirit baptism. Begin teaching them the scriptures about Jesus and the importance of fellowship.

2. *Redeem the body.* The soul lives in, and therefore needs, the body. Teach the new disciples that the body is the temple of the Holy Spirit. Instruct them about taking

care of their health. (It is remarkable how many church leaders I meet with that have high blood pressure and/ or type II diabetes—both symptoms of stress and poor diet.) Talk frankly about health issues like addiction to alcohol, drugs, prescription medications etc. Teach them that their body is now the temple of the Holy Spirit.

3. *Redeem the finances.* Our physical lives need finances. For most, the issue is not greed, but lack of stewardship. Jesus needs to come and overhaul our finances. So, we discuss topics like being a good and faithful worker; debt; and bad financial principles resulting in bad decisions. Are they saving? Are they generous? Paul addressed these issues with those he disciple (e.g. 2 Thess 3; 1 Tim 5:8). Financial bondage is a huge issue in the world and, sadly, all too often in the church.

4. *Redeem the relationships.* This is an area that will always need attention. We must regularly ask the disciple direct questions: Are you demonstrating love to your spouse? Are you giving your children your time and attention? Are you caring for your parents? Are you making room for neighbors and strangers? We need to teach disciples to bless their enemies by praying for them, by returning their anger with gentleness and forgiveness. Jesus told us to "Do good to those that hate you" (Mt 5:44 KJV), calling us up to the higher plain of loving actions. In this way, our enemy becomes our neighbor and friend; from here we can introduce him or her to Jesus. Jesus never treated anyone as an enemy; therefore, we have no right

to have enemies in this world. Loving our neighbor is very practical. When we can:

- Pray for our neighbor
- Bless our neighbor
- Forgive our neighbor
- Do good to our neighbor

—then we truly love our neighbor. These are vital discipleship lessons that will impact our entire lives as the Lord continues to bring new neighbors into our lives; and a neighbor can be *anyone*, and not just the person we live beside.

5. *Redeem others.* Teach them the truth and power of 2 Tim 2:2. Disciple others who will, in turn, disciple others. Take your disciple with you. Let them watch how you disciple others so that they, in turn, can do the same.

These five areas give us a specific focus in making disciples, helping us to be intentional and deliberate. Notice how practical these five areas are, touching all the critical areas of the disciple's life. Notice, too, that this very focused approach connects us back to one of the keys that Jesus demonstrated: the power of a shared life. This kind of discipleship cannot take place in a classroom; it happens in the natural give and take of doing life together. It is built on love and trust. This approach doesn't allow us to hide behind the "spiritual" topics and thereby avoid the real issues of people's lives. Jesus always dealt with people compassionately, but directly, whether it was the woman who had been married five times or the rich man who was too attached to his belongings. After so many decades pastoring and in ministry, it would be too easy for me to get discouraged by the moral failings of leaders and followers, the financial scandals, the marital train wrecks. But I am convinced that these are symptoms of doing church instead of making disciples. The pain and destruction are *not* inevitable. The answer is a vibrant, authentic, corporate life of committed discipleship with brothers and sisters who are learning to truly follow Jesus.

> *"Therefore, since we are surrounded by such a great cloud of witnesses, let us throw off everything that hinders and the sin that so easily entangles, and let us run with perseverance the race marked out for us. Let us fix our eyes on Jesus, the author and perfecter of our faith."*
>
> *(Heb 12:1-2 NIV)*

14

It's Time

"And He sent them out."

Luke 9:2

There is something unsettling about leaving what is known and embarking on the unfamiliar. And that is why most people never make the journey. But following Jesus has always meant entering the unknown. Abraham, who Paul calls "the father of the faith," didn't clearly know where he was headed, but he was convinced that God had spoken. Even more, Abraham knew that what he had heard required a response. Deep down, Abraham believed that there was more—much more—to life.

> *"Abraham was confidently looking forward to a city with eternal foundations, a city designed and built by God."*
>
> *(Heb 11:10 NLT)*

He was entering a new kind of life in a new place, but somehow

Abraham knew this life would be, at least to some degree, a reflection of an eternal city. It was the same for the early church. They responded to God's call to live by the standard and supernatural life of the Age to Come. In this way, they became a truly prophetic people who chose to live "Heaven now."

This determination to follow Jesus' call did not come without cost: they were misunderstood, criticized and lied about. The early church shared their material goods, often out of necessity as the believers were discriminated against socially and economically. During the first three hundred years, the church lived through times of persecution and danger. So why did they choose to follow Christ? They had seen the awesome reality of Christ and had glimpsed eternity as it impacted their lives in the here and now. These believers had experienced the joy, abundance and deep love that God had always intended for them. They were part of a new kind of community, and they wouldn't trade anything for it.

All over the world, disciples have discovered the same truth today. This abundant, joyful life of loving Jesus and one another is the treasure in the field; for this discovery, they have given everything—and in doing so, they have *gained* everything that really matters. When I first encountered believers living like this, I wrote home to my wife. I did not write about the remarkable growth of these churches that met in homes. I didn't even write about the many miracles that I witnessed, or their amazing commitment to Christ. Instead, what I wrote was this: *I have met the most joyful Christians that I have ever encountered.*

Jesus gave every one of us a great purpose: The Great Commission. This is our assignment, to be followed not in *our* way, but *His*. As we do so, our lives quickly move from the realm of ideas and concepts to the fruitfulness of formation and multiplication. The beauty of this assignment is that it is fulfilled in the midst of life together, where we discover the joy of what Jesus called abundant life. Everyone is made for joy and love. No wonder First Churches are growing faster than any time in history; it is almost irresistibly attractive.

You have all you need to move forward. Yes, it will mean leaving what is familiar, but following Jesus always means leaving something behind. I have sought to make this book as practical and concrete as possible. I encourage you to look carefully at the *Putting It into Practice* sections that are at the end of most chapters. But don't stop there; make a commitment to activate what you are reading. Keep going. It takes time to establish new patterns. As you establish a First Church, review some of the key principles. Here are just a few:

- Everyone was created for family, no one was created for meetings.

- Belonging comes before believing.

- Gospel is always inclusive.

- Disciples make disciples.

- It is a "go" gospel.

- Discipling happens through teaching, imitation and welcome.

- Eat together. A lot.

With all that is in my heart, I urge you to embark on this journey. There is nothing else you need to know.

It's time.

> *"They shared meals together with joyful hearts and tender humility. They were continually filled with praises to God, enjoying the favor of all the people. And the Lord kept adding to their number daily those who were coming to life."*
>
> *(Act 2:46-47 TPT)*

ACKNOWEDGEMENTS

The writing of any book involves many more people than just the author, including those who edit, critique, encourage, and contribute new ideas; *The First Church Restored* is no exception. I once heard a well-known Bible teacher say that a book is a great investment because it contains the author's life message which was forged over many years. In a very real way, this book has been formed by the hundreds of teachers, writers, pastors, and friends who I have known over the years of my walk with Jesus.

Thanks to Steve Dragswolf who helped me with the structure of this book and its chapters. Your insights helped me to communicate with more precision. Thanks to Don Cleverley who, once again, painstakingly went through every word of the manuscript. Don, your capacity for detailed accuracy is amazing. Thanks to Tim Stewart who did the final read-through and set the design and layout for the book. Your artistic eye is a gift from the Lord. Steve Sjogren, thanks for reading this book and writing the foreword. I am thankful for our thirty years of ministry history.

Thank you to all those who prayed for me during the many months I worked on the book. Thanks especially to Sue Walker for your prayer and for organizing the prayer covering that I and Impact Nations enjoy from men and women all over the world. Sue, thanks for your many years of encouragement and support. You have helped me to keep growing in my understanding of the centrality of a prayer foundation for any endeavor. My thanks to all those in Albuquerque who so faithfully continue to pray for me.

This book would not have been possible without Randeep and Anu Mathews. Although you call me Dad, it is you that I have learned so much from. In the pages of this book, you will recognize much of what you have shared with me over the years. What you have allowed the Lord to do through your faithful obedience is remarkable. Thank you for your example and inspiration. Thank you, too, for your willingness to go to other nations on my behalf, teaching others what you have taught me. Thank you for bringing me into your spiritual family. As I told Christina after spending time with all of you, all those years ago: "I have just found the most joyful Christians I have ever met." The same is true today.

Thank you to my friend, Anuroop Swamy for your wisdom and insights, especially as they relate to how disciples are formed. Thank you for introducing me to a whole network of men and women who have discovered treasure, both old and new.

When Impact Nations began in 2004, I never dreamed of how far it would reach, or all that we would be able to do to holistically rescue lives by bringing supernatural and practical expressions of God's Kingdom. As Dorothy Day used to say, "All is grace." One of the greatest unexpected blessings of this great adventure has been the family that Jesus has formed. I have family all over the world, men and women who are deeply committed to living the Gospel. Thank you to all our national partners who work so tirelessly around the developing world, laying down their lives, day after day, for the love of God and people. You are my heroes.

Thank you to the hundreds and hundreds of people who sacrifice their time, energy, vacations and finances in order to travel with me and others on Journeys of Compassion. Thank you to those courageous people who, usually with no warning, drop everything and fly into disaster areas immediately following earthquakes, hurricanes and typhoons in order to bring safe drinking water and medical care.

Thank you to my family who continue to encourage me to keep following Jesus, even when it means time apart from my children and grandchildren. No matter where I am in the world, I carry you in my heart. More than any other person, I thank you Christina. As we head toward five decades together, you continue to be my best friend and the love of my life. I am so proud of you, and like all who know you, I am amazed by your energy and steadfastness.

Finally, thank you my Lord Jesus. You have always been faithful to me in every way. I love You more than I ever have before; may my love continue to grow into all eternity.

IMPACT NATIONS

Founded in 2005, Impact Nations partners with leaders in the developing world to rescue lives and transform communities by engaging people in practical and supernatural expressions of the Kingdom of God.

We accomplish our mission primarily through three types of activity:
- Journeys of Compassion
- Clean Water Projects
- Skills and Business Training

To learn more about Impact Nations and how you can get involved, contact us:

1-877-736-0803
www.impactnations.com
info@impactnations.com

PO Box 45596
Rio Rancho, NM 87124

Don't miss the

IMPACT NATIONS PODCAST

Steve provides in depth teaching that opens up the scriptures
and gives practical application for today. He also interviews
other theologians and authors.

You can listen or subscribe at:

www.impactnations.com/podcast

MORE FROM STEVE STEWART

WHEN EVERYTHING CHANGES:
Healing, Justice & the Kingdom of God

The Kingdom of God is bigger, more powerful and more inclusive than we ever imagined. Jesus Christ delcared a gospel that is radical in its scope and implications, and power enough to bring change to everything it touches.

THE JOURNEY:
35 Stories of Kingdom Encounters

Take a Journey through 35 stories spanninig 25 years and five continents, each one life changing. Steve shares his experiences with a God who is always on the move, rescuing lives and surprising us with His miraculous, extravagant love.

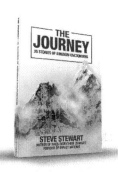

DOING THE GOSPEL:
Learning to Walk in the Rhythm of the Kingdom

You were created to live a life filled with Kingdom activity. This five hour video series and accompanying workbook will teach you to see the Kingdom of God powerfully released in your community. Discover how easy it is to effectively heal the sick and lead people to Jesus.

BOOK AN IMPACT WEEKEND

Are you looking for a fresh release of Kingdom activity in your community? Host Steve for a life-changing weekend!

Steve teaches scriptural principles, always with an emphasis on practical application. His goal is that people go home not only with more understanding, but more faith and tangible experience than when they arrived. He does this through demonstration and activation/participation. During an *Impact Weekend*, Steve teaches, then provides opportunities for all participants to immediately engage in healing ministry – he takes people out into the community to pray for the sick, share the Gospel and minister to the poor.

Topics include:
- Understanding, Experiencing, and Releasing the Kingdom of God
- The Compassionate Jesus
- Keys to Healing
- Following Jesus
- Justice, the Poor, and the Revolutionary Gospel of Jesus
- The Unsearchable Riches of Christ
- The Power of Inclusion

To to learn more about planning an Impact Weekend in your community, contact us at:

info@impactnations.com
or
1-877-736-0803

Made in the USA
Columbia, SC
03 August 2020